THE ENGLISH
COUNTRY HOUSE

JAMES PEILL

FOREWORD BY
JULIAN FELLOWES

PHOTOGRAPHS BY
JAMES FENNELL

THE VENDOME PRESS
NEW YORK

CONTENTS

Foreword

JULIAN FELLOWES

The English country house has long held a fascination for people from all over the world and is a subject that never fails to reward an investigation into its rites and customs. It is fairly common knowledge that I have long been interested in country houses and the stories of their occupants, the families who once owned them, as well as the men and women who worked in them, and it is consequently exciting to discover houses hitherto unknown to me and learn about their history with that intriguing blend of great art and architecture mixed in with the romance and tragedy of the people who have lived within their walls.

The ten houses in this book all have a fascinating story to tell and they are the more remarkable for only ever having passed by inheritance since the day they were built. A house that has never been sold tells a complete and unbroken story in a way that is virtually impossible to replicate in a house that has changed hands. The lives of the owners' forebears are present on every side, not only in their portraits hanging on the walls, but also in the more mundane everyday items: old trunks and suitcases in the attic, jewelled seals in vitrine cases, bundled letters tied with ribbon, old photograph albums and visitors' books, family pedigrees on torn and faded vellum, well-worn silver, cracked china, and faded chintz curtains. These are some of the things that James Peill and I recently pored over at Goodwood as we filmed a documentary delving into the histories of some of the people who had lived and worked in the house. That is what this book is about, celebrating not just the families who have created these lovely places over the centuries but also their employees who have helped them to do it. The gardeners who have tended the Hackthorn vine, reputedly the second oldest in the country after the one at Hampton Court, are just such a case in point.

James has picked a fascinating selection of houses; they range from two great stately homes that will be well known to many (Badminton and Goodwood) to some smaller and lesser-known houses, such as Kentchurch and Hackthorn, that epitomize the gentler kind of country house, more modest perhaps than the palaces of great noblemen, but in many ways more enviable for that. We must be grateful to the owners for allowing us such an intimate glimpse of their homes; only half of the houses in this book are open to the public and some have never featured in a published work before. I like the fact that James has included five churches or chapels in this book, for the story of the country house cannot be separated from the history of the Church in this country. It is within these places of worship that so many key moments in the lives of previous generations took place and their memorials serve as visual reminders of people and times long gone.

This book has been brought to life by the superb photographs of James Fennell, himself no stranger to country house life as his own home appeared in his previous collaboration with James Peill, *The Irish Country House*. James has managed to capture the special atmosphere of generations of one family's occupation that pervades these houses. His use of natural lighting helps to transport us into each house and to discover the layers of its history.

The surge of interest in the English country house that has followed in the wake of *Downton Abbey* demonstrates, I hope anyway, how genuinely interested people are in this aspect of our nation's history. I am sure that this book will give great pleasure to any who open its covers.

Introduction

The country houses of England are among her crowning glories. Famous throughout the world, they have been studied and written about for centuries. Travel writers such as Celia Fiennes in the early eighteenth century and Prince Pückler-Muskau in the nineteenth, along with authors such as Jane Austen, the Brontë sisters, and Maria Edgeworth helped fuel the English romance with the country house. In these periods, books were written about the history of ancient family seats and the lineage of their owners, accompanied by charming engravings of rural idylls. The advent of photography brought with it a new wave of interest in country houses, most vividly seen in the magazine *Country Life* along with its landmark publications such as Charles Latham's *In English Homes* series. More recently, the subject has been explored in great depth, spearheaded by Mark Girouard's *Life in the English Country House*, first published in 1978 and still in print.

The present book, rather than being an exhaustive study of the English country house per se, is a personal selection of ten houses that have passed by inheritance through the generations, in some cases for nearly a thousand years. The houses have been chosen as representative of both larger and smaller houses from different periods, ranging from medieval times to the early twentieth century. The fact that they have never been sold means that each one has a particular character and atmosphere related to the lives of the family that has lived within its walls. The photographs do a wonderful job of capturing these layers of history.

As Mark Girouard explains at the start of his book, country houses were essentially power houses, the homes of a ruling class who exerted influence at the local and national levels. The ownership of land was the key ingredient in exercising this power, and with it came status. Vital in sending out the appropriate message of that status was the architecture of the country house, the evolution of which can be followed to a greater or lesser extent through the houses in this book. Like many country houses, most of them have had alterations over the centuries, but one significant architectural phase usually predominates.

The medieval Kentchurch Court, hidden in the Welsh Marches, was built as a fortified manor house entered through an archway in a protective curtain wall dating from the fourteenth century. Medieval houses were centered on a great hall, where the entire household congregated to eat, owner and servants alike. The kitchen and chapel usually formed the other rooms. Over time the eating arrangements changed, and by the end of the sixteenth century, the owner and his family no longer ate with their household in the great hall but tended to dine in private in rooms or chambers that led off of it.

The need for defense gradually diminished and the fifteenth century saw advances in technology that enabled the mass production of brick. It was used to build the early gatehouse at Madresfield Court in Worcestershire (a house originally—and still—surrounded by a moat). Symmetrical Tudor palaces with elaborate brickwork sprang up; clusters of chimneys became works of art using cut and moulded bricks. Brick was often combined with flint or timbered construction and distinct regional variations were seen across the country.

The influence of the Italian Renaissance really began to be felt at the beginning of the sixteenth century and reached its peak in England in the Elizabethan era, when the great prodigy houses such as Burghley, Longleat, Hardwick Hall, and Hatfield House were built. It was during Elizabeth I's reign that Prideaux Place was built by Sir Nicholas Prideaux in an E-shaped form, a plan that can be seen used all over the country. Like many country houses that rose up after Henry VIII's Dissolution of the Monasteries in the sixteenth century, the house was probably built on monastic foundations. Its wonderful great chamber on the first floor, crowned by a magnificent plasterwork ceiling, would have been used for banquets and dancing, while a parlour would have served for more informal entertaining. Milton was also built during the reign of Elizabeth I, its north front composed of huge bay windows with stone mullions and centered by a classical porch with two tiers of columns. Larger houses often had a long gallery, designed primarily for the taking of exercise; when it was situated on the top floor, it also afforded pleasing views over the surrounding landscape.

Gabled bays were a feature of some Elizabethan houses but became one of the main characteristics of Jacobean country houses, particularly Dutch gables with their distinctively shaped outline. The original houses at both Goodwood and Hackthorn, now seen only in contemporary paintings, had symmetrical fronts with gabled ends.

The influence of the Italian architect Andrea Palladio and his book *I quattro libri dell'architettura* began to be felt in England in the early decades of the seventeenth century, particularly in the design and plans of Inigo Jones's classical buildings such as the Queen's House, Greenwich, and the Banqueting House, Whitehall. Palladio preached strict adherence to the rules of classical architecture as originally drawn up by the Roman architect Vitruvius.

The Restoration of Charles II inevitably brought with it French ideas and tastes, as many members of the court had lived in exile in France with the king. One of these was the Earl of Arlington, who built his new seat at Euston in Norfolk in the French manner, with a central court and large pavilions at each corner; although it was later subsumed by Matthew Brettingham's alterations, it forms the focal point in a hunting painting by Thomas Wyck. Inigo Jones's Prince's Lodging in nearby Newmarket was almost certainly the prototype for the red brick, often astylar, country houses of the Restoration period. Smaller country houses that belonged to the gentry sprang up all over England during this period and into the eighteenth century.

The dawn of the eighteenth century saw the rise of the baroque style in England, most notably in the architecture of Sir Christopher Wren and his pupils Nicholas Hawksmoor and William Talman. Hawksmoor worked with the supremely talented architect and playwright Sir John Vanbrugh at Castle Howard and Blenheim Palace, while Talman was the architect of Chatsworth, and in this book, the stable block at Milton. Wren also had a strong influence on James Gibbs, who was one of several notable architects involved at Badminton following on from Francis Smith of Warwick. Gibbs also put forward proposals for modernizing Milton in 1726.

Colen Campbell's *Vitruvius Britannicus*, which appeared in three volumes between 1715 and 1725, marked a return to more correct classicism and the influence of Palladio. William Kent was one of the greatest proponents of the revived Palladian style together with the talented Maecenas Richard Boyle, third Earl of Burlington. Kent took over from Gibbs at Badminton, designing the two-tier pediment crowning the north front and its flanking cupolas. Lord Burlington probably introduced Kent to the second Duke of Grafton, for whom Kent sketched designs for a new house at Euston. Even though the new house was never executed, the genius of Kent's architecture can be seen in his splendid banqueting house at Euston, known as the Temple. Although the rococo style did not become a significant phase in English architecture, it can be seen in the superb plasterwork executed during this period, for example in the hall and octagonal anteroom at Badminton.

Matthew Brettingham was one of Kent's protégés and his work can be seen at both Euston Hall and Goodwood House. He gave Euston a Palladian makeover and at Goodwood added the pedimented family wing. Like Gibbs, he also submitted plans for modernizing Milton, but these came to nothing. In the end, it was Henry Flitcroft, another of Kent's protégés, who remodeled Milton and designed an entirely new south façade in the Palladian style. As so often happened in country house building, the death of his employer, the third Earl Fitzwilliam, meant that Flitcroft's work was never completed and it was left to another great architect to finish the job: Sir William Chambers. Along with Robert Adam and James Wyatt, Chambers was one of the greatest neoclassical architects of the second half of the eighteenth century. His work can also be seen at Goodwood, where he designed the grand stable block. Wyatt was employed at Goodwood as well and was responsible for the neoclassical Tapestry Drawing Room, the only room to survive from his (now demolished) north wing.

Country house builders all over England embraced the new neoclassical style. Hackthorn Hall, designed by neoclassical architect James Lewis for a traditional country squire, is typical of the neoclassical "villas" set in well-wooded parks that could be seen up and down the country.

Of course, the landscape surrounding a country house was just as important as the house itself; each supported the other. Early landscapes were composed along formal lines, with vistas radiating out from the house, through formal gardens, and over the surrounding countryside, as seen in early depictions of Badminton and Euston Hall. However, influenced by the paintings of Claude Lorrain and Nicolas Poussin, the eighteenth century saw the rise of the naturalistic landscaped park, led by William Kent and Charles Bridgeman and ultimately seen in the work of Lancelot "Capability" Brown and his successor, Humphry Repton. The latter was employed at Milton in the 1790s.

The picturesque movement, which took place toward the end of the eighteenth century, was a reaction against the strict formality of neoclassicism and Brown's idealized landscapes. It is perfectly encapsulated in John Nash's Gothic alterations to the medieval Kentchurch Court and its position at the foot of Garway Hill on the Welsh Marches. Alterations were also carried out at Prideaux Place in "Strawberry Hill Gothic," named after Horace Walpole's Thames-side villa. Gothic architecture was seen as a suitable style for families of ancient lineage, their arms emblazoned in stained-glass windows.

During the Regency period, with its emphasis on comfort, a mixture of styles was in vogue. James Wyatt worked at Goodwood in the Egyptian, picturesque, and neoclassical styles. Regency mock castles, like Eastnor Castle in Herefordshire, sprang up throughout the land; grand series of reception rooms were cloaked on the exterior with crenellated turrets and rooflines and all the trappings of a medieval castle.

The Victorian period saw a revival of earlier architectural styles, particularly the Gothic. Seen as the national style, it was associated with both Christianity and truthfulness; one of its greatest protagonists was Augustus W. N. Pugin. Madresfield Court, having been altered several times in its long history, was rebuilt yet again in the fashionable "Jacobethan" style (a mixture of Elizabethan and Jacobean styles) by Philip Hardwick. Some Victorian houses were a complete hybrid of styles; Inwood has elements of Jacobean, Scottish Baronial, classical, and chinoiserie architecture all rolled into one.

In the last decades of the nineteenth century, the Arts and Crafts movement took off, rejecting the mass production of the Industrial Revolution and preaching a return to traditional craftsmanship and values. Rodmarton Manor and Madresfield Court (the Library and Chapel) are possibly two of the finest expressions of Arts and Crafts theory in the country, where every element of the architecture and furnishings combine to form a perfect union.

All of the houses in this book are at the center of landed estates whose presence has shaped, to a greater or lesser extent, the surrounding landscape. Sport has played a vital role in that shaping, particularly game shooting and fox hunting; Badminton and Milton still have their own hunt kennels. Each house is supported by a range of ancillary buildings necessary for the running of the house and estate, and accommodation for some of those who are employed at it. Many of the houses have either a chapel or a church within their grounds, illustrating the central importance of Christianity in the lives of the families who lived and worked there. Indeed, for hundreds of years, society in many ways reflected the Divine Order. The church is also a place where successive generations are most vividly recalled with family monuments, inscribed memorials, tombstones, and commemorative stained-glass windows, many often decorated with the family coat of arms. Heraldry also plays a role in the decoration of the house itself, proclaiming the family's status and ownership on everything from tablets above the entrance door to silver teaspoons on the table.

A common legacy of one family's ownership of a house for generations is an art collection, whether as a natural consequence of general accumulation or as the result of specific collecting, on the Grand Tour, for example. Several of the houses in the book possess outstanding collections of art, whereas others have the more typical collection of family portraits hung on the walls, ephemera in the attics, and furniture and silver still being used in day-to-day life. Badminton boasts a particularly complete group of family portraits.

The families that own the houses featured in the book range from the upper echelons of the aristocracy to members of the landed gentry. All have served their king and country at various levels: as county councillors, Justices of the Peace, High Sheriffs, Lord Lieutenants, Members of Parliament and of the House of Lords, positions at Court and in the Royal Household, and service in the Army, Royal Navy, and more recently, Royal Air Force. Many younger sons joined the Church or entered the Colonial Service. Primogeniture has played its part in preserving the houses and estates intact.

The mere survival of these houses and estates into the twenty-first century must be lauded. The agricultural depression toward the end of the nineteenth century, combined with crippling taxation, fear of the future, and the devastation of the two world wars in the twentieth century, dealt a deathblow to many English country houses, particularly those belonging to members of the landed gentry. Adam Nicolson, in his recent book *The Gentry*, estimates that until 1914 the gentry (as opposed to the aristocracy) owned half of England; now they own less than 1 percent. Between 1945 and 1955, nearly a thousand country houses were demolished, the full scale of the destruction only realized when the landmark exhibition *The Destruction of the Country House* was held at the Victoria and Albert Museum in 1974.

All of the families and their houses in this book have had to adapt to the twenty-first century. It is exciting to see how each has responded to the challenges thrown at them, many in very innovative ways. For example, the Badminton Horse Trials and the Goodwood Festival of Speed are now two of the most famous sporting events in the world and go a long way toward ensuring the survival of their respective estates. The romance of the English country house never ceases to appeal, whether it is through literature or film, and this book serves to illustrate one of our nation's greatest legacies.

Kentchurch Court

HEREFORDSHIRE

A portrait of the Scudamores' mystical tutor, Jack of Kent, dating from about 1460, has a view of Kentchurch in the background— it is the earliest known depiction of an English country house. Legends abound concerning Jack of Kent and his magical powers; he is reputed to have lived until he was 120.

Kentchurch is buried deep in the Welsh Marches, the ancient borderland between England and Wales, surrounded by a myriad of high-hedged country lanes and wooded escarpments. The approach could not be more romantic: a lane winds past the now-unused Gothic lodge with portcullis gates, swings round near the little church, and leads straight down a secluded valley with park railings on one side and woods on the other. As a castellated tower looms into view, the drive passes through a pair of great wrought-iron gates, their piers topped by roaring heraldic bears holding shields. Traversing the stable yard, the drive continues through a Gothic archway in the curtain wall, bringing the visitor to rest beside a crenellated entrance porch at the front of the house, facing out over the deer park that rises beyond to the bracken-covered slopes of Garway Hill.

There is an all-pervading feeling of antiquity at Kentchurch, which has been the home of the Scudamore family for nearly a thousand years. Early records of the family are scarce and intertwined with myth and legend. According to Burke's *Landed Gentry*, the first of the family to be described as "of Kentchurch" is Sir John Scudamore, Knight, descended from Sir Alan Scudamore, Knight,

who was living in 1091. Sir John lived in the second half of the fourteenth and early fifteenth century and was married to Alice, daughter of the famous Welsh prince Owen Glendower, who had led an unsuccessful rebellion against the English. Family tradition holds that he took refuge in the tower at Kentchurch following the collapse of his revolt around 1412, although his final years remain a mystery.

PRECEDING PAGES: *Climbing roses tumble over Gothic windows and a little door on the east front of Kentchurch.*

OPPOSITE: *The entrance arch, with its heavy, studded oak doors, dates from the fourteenth century and is part of the original fortifications.*

LEFT: *A heraldic stone bear roars atop one of the gate piers.*

OVERLEAF: *Kentchurch lies hidden in a secluded valley on the border between England and Wales. The Black Mountains can be glimpsed in the distance.*

Kentchurch was built originally as a fortified manor house. The earliest surviving part of the house is the buttressed entrance archway, with its massive, studded doors, which is believed to date from the mid-fourteenth century. The three lower storeys of the tower (in which Owen Glendower hid) probably date from the latter part of

that century. A portrait of the Scudamores' mystical tutor, Jack of Kent, dating from about 1460, has a view of Kentchurch in the background—it is the earliest known depiction of an English country house. Legends abound concerning Jack of Kent and his magical powers; he is reputed to have lived until he was 120.

By the eighteenth century, the house had grown and incorporated late-seventeenth- and early-eighteenth-century additions, including hipped roofs and tall chimneys. A watercolour from that time shows the windows of the medieval great hall still at the heart of the house. The archway is barely visible beneath a Dutch-gabled garrison and the tower has a pyramidal roof.

In 1773 the squire of the day, Colonel John Scudamore, decided to make improvements to his ancient family seat and employed Anthony Keck, a talented neoclassical architect with an extensive local practice. Keck was tasked with remodeling the interior for Colonel Scudamore's wife, who had taken a fancy to the "old and irregular" building. He introduced a long corridor, or "gallery," off of which three reception rooms open: a dining room, drawing room, and library. In the final years of the eighteenth century, Colonel Scudamore focused his attention on the exterior of the house and as Keck was by now rather elderly, he approached John Nash to carry out the designs. Unfortunately, Colonel Scudamore died the following year, before work could have been completed, but his portrait shows him holding a rough sketch of designs for the house. He was probably introduced to Nash by his friend Uvedale Price, a neighboring Herefordshire landowner and one of the earliest proponents of the picturesque movement. Nash's alterations are likely those seen in an early-nineteenth-century painting of the house and include heightening the tower and giving

it a circular staircase turret. The main body of the house was encased asymmetrically and given Gothic windows and a castellated roofline. On the north side of the house he added a huge "chapel" window, complete with pinnacled buttress, that joined the tower with one of the earlier ranges. This chapel window is purely a conceit; inside it forms the dramatic finale to the "gallery" that runs the length of the building, ending in a short flight of stairs that rises to the "sanctuary" below the window.

Just over twenty years later, Colonel Scudamore's grandson John Lucy Scudamore inherited the house; while he was on the Grand Tour with his bride, Sarah, further alterations were made, this time overseen by the agent Thomas Tudor and supervised by Sarah's father, Sir Harford Jones. Tudor seems to have acted as his own architect and it appears he altered the east front to create two larger reception rooms and a new entrance porch. His range, with large sash windows beneath hood, or label, moulds, complements Nash's east range with its Gothic tracery windows. Sandwiched between these two ranges is an early example of the Norman Revival. On the ground floor of this section is the library, which has a triple-arched, columned screen.

OPPOSITE: *Grinling Gibbons carving from Holme Lacy hangs over the mantelpiece in the library.*

TOP LEFT: *The east front, which was altered by Thomas Tudor, agent at Kentchurch in the 1820s.*

BOTTOM LEFT: *The screen of arches and columns in the library, dating from the 1820s, is an early example of Norman Revival decoration. When the flood swept through the house in 1959, old Mrs. Lucas-Scudamore took refuge atop one of the bookcases.*

OVERLEAF: *The dining room is hung with a fine collection of family portraits, including a pregnant Lady Packington to the right of the chimneypiece.*

A glimpse of this façade can be seen in
Colonel Scudamore's portrait.

Despite its hidden location, Kentchurch
has not been immune to the ravages of time
and misfortune. At the end of the nineteenth
century, many of the Kentchurch treasures
were taken over to Castle Shane, the Lucas
family seat in Ireland (John Lucy Scudamore's
only child, Laura, had married Major
Fitzherbert Lucas in 1852). Unfortunately,
Shane was burnt during the Troubles in 1920,
and many of the Kentchurch heirlooms were
destroyed. However, the marriage of Laura's
grandson Jack to Lady Patricia Scudamore-
Stanhope, only daughter of the twelfth (and
last) Earl of Chesterfield, brought with it
many new treasures, including the famous
ornamental carvings by Grinling Gibbons
that had formerly graced the walls at Holme

Lacy in Herefordshire. Holme Lacy had been
the seat of another branch of the Scudamore
family and had passed by inheritance to
the Earls of Chesterfield. Lady Patricia's
marriage thus reunited the two branches
of the family after five and a half centuries
of separation. When Lady Patricia's great-
uncle the tenth Earl of Chesterfield died, a
big sale was held of the contents of his home,
Beningborough Hall, near York. Included
in that sale were many Scudamore family
portraits originally from Holme Lacy, and
Lady Patricia and her husband bought them.
Thus, the walls of Kentchurch are now
hung with family portraits dating back to
the sixteenth century. The dining room, a
large, classically proportioned room with
coved cornice, has a superb pair of full-
length Elizabethan portraits of Sir John and
Lady Packington. Sir John was called "Lusty
Packington" by Queen Elizabeth I, who
took a fancy to him and brought him to her
court. His wife, who appears pregnant in her
portrait, was a rich widow and heiress, but
the marriage was not a happy one; she was
said to have been "a violent little lady," and
they separated in 1607. The "sanctuary" is
overlooked by another striking Elizabethan

portrait, this one of Sir James Scudamore, resplendent in tilt armour (the armour is now in the Metropolitan Museum, New York). Renowned for his tilting skills and a legendary figure in Elizabeth's court, he is said to have been the inspiration for Edmund Spenser's "Scudamour," a gallant knight in *The Faerie Queen*. The name is a pun on "L'escu d'amour" the Anglo-Norman origin of his surname, which means "shield of love."

Lady Patricia's husband, Lieutenant-Commander Jack Lucas-Scudamore, was a brilliant raconteur with a great sense of humour and still fondly remembered by those who knew him. He was the first student at Oxford University to own a motorcar and once, when banned from driving, dressed up as his mother, took her passport and driving license, and drove to France for the season. His mother, Sybil, was a great friend of the playwright and novelist George Bernard Shaw, who was a regular visitor to Kentchurch.

St James Scudamore
Father of
John 1.st L.st Viscount
Scudamore

OPPOSITE TOP: *The downstairs cloakroom is hung with a medley of old prints.*

OPPOSITE BOTTOM: *Gardening tools artistically arranged in the shed.*

TOP LEFT: *The gallant Sir James Scudamore, dressed in armour for the Accession Day Tilt, attributed to Marcus Gheeraerts the Younger.*

BOTTOM LEFT: *George Bernard Shaw at Kentchurch.*

BELOW: *Books salvaged from the floodwaters more than fifty years ago.*

OVERLEAF: *The gardens and grounds of Kentchurch are filled with flora and fauna. A medieval oak tree survives in the deer park.*

In May 1959 tragedy struck again when a storm turned the stream that runs behind the house into a raging torrent. It poured down the narrow valley and into the house, bringing with it timber that had just been felled. Water cascaded down the "sanctuary" steps and broke open doors as it surged forward. Old Mrs. Lucas-Scudamore, who was in the library at the time, had to take refuge atop the bookcases, while the sheer force of the water ripped the stove out of the wall and carried it clear across the kitchen. The high-water mark in the dining room was 5 feet 4 inches (a plaque records this). It took three years to restore the house and contents.

Today, Kentchurch is the home of Johnny and Jan Lucas-Scudamore and their (now-grown-up) children, who have valiantly restored much of the house and its remarkable contents. Their efforts have begun to pay dividends as people begin to realize the importance of this lesser known of English country houses.

Prideaux Place

CORNWALL

ith its ribbed, Gothic-vaulted ceiling and stained-glass window imparting an atmospheric "gloomth," the architecture of the library recalls Horace Walpole's famous Strawberry Hill. The many heiresses who have married into the family are recalled through the riot of heraldry in the stained-glass windows, and the shelves are stacked two books deep with a collection of over six thousand volumes.

The Prideaux family has been seated at Prideaux Place for more than four hundred years, but their ties with Cornwall go back almost a thousand years, to the time of the Norman Conquest in 1066, when they were recorded as Lords of Prideaux Castle at Luxulyan. "Place," as it was known for much of its history, presides over the north coastal town of Padstow and has distant views of the Camel Estuary. Fallow deer graze in the ancient deer park; legend has it that if the deer die out, so does the Prideaux family.

According to family tradition, Sir Nicholas Prideaux completed the house in 1592. He had his great-uncle, another Nicholas Prideaux, to thank for his lucrative inheritance; a shrewd lawyer, Great-uncle Nicholas had advised the Prior of Bodmin, who feared that Henry VIII might soon close down the priory and seize its lands, to give a long lease of the

lands of Padstow to the prior's niece. He then arranged the marriage between the prior's niece and his own nephew and heir, William Prideaux. Finally, against all odds, Nicholas won a legal action against Henry VIII and managed to buy the freehold of the lands, thus securing them for his own family.

The house erected by Sir Nicholas, like so many Elizabethan manor houses, was E-shaped, with pointed gables joined by a crenellated roofline. The house can be seen in an early-eighteenth-century oil painting with formal gardens to the south and the fishing harbour in the foreground. This "new and stately house," as it was described by Richard Carew in his *Survey of Cornwall* (1602), forms the nucleus of the present-day house. Although little of Sir Nicholas's interior remains, it must have been fitted out to a very high standard, as the marquetry

PRECEDING PAGES: *Prideaux Place wakes up from its slumbers, caught in the early morning light. A flight of stone steps leads up to the Gothic window of the library.*

OPPOSITE: *The staircase was created in about 1810 for the Reverend Charles Prideaux-Brune.*

LEFT, TOP TO BOTTOM: *Liberal use is made of heraldry at Prideaux Place: the Prideaux arms above the front door; a bell button in the dining room with the goat crest of the Brunes; the Prideaux shield painted on the back of a hall chair.*

ABOVE: *Originally the
great hall, the dining room
dates back to the eighteenth
century. Its walls are
covered with a mixture of
Elizabethan and Georgian
paneling. It was badly dam-
aged by fire in the late nineteenth century. A portrait
of Sir Nicholas Prideaux,
builder of the house, hangs
over the fireplace.*

OPPOSITE TOP LEFT AND
RIGHT: *Details of the
sixteenth-century
marquetry paneling in the
dining room.*

OPPOSITE BOTTOM LEFT
AND RIGHT: *Details of
oak furniture in the dining
room, including a panel
carved with the shield of
the Brune family.*

paneling in the great hall, now used as the
dining room, attests. Above the fireplace
hangs a portrait of Sir Nicholas attributed
to Marcus Gheeraerts the Younger, showing
him wearing a high ruff. The house was
inherited by Sir Nicholas's son John, who
was probably responsible for the magnificent
great chamber on the first floor, with its
soaring, canted, plaster ceiling covered in
a complex design of strapwork framing
flowers, animals, and scenes from the story
of Susannah and the Elders (as found in the
Apocrypha). Two pendant bosses hang almost
as if suspended in mid-air; a huge panel at
the northern end depicts Moses at the well,
while the southern end boasts the armorial
achievement of the present squire as a
Knight of Malta, made to commemorate the
restoration of the room in 1987. For much of
its later history the room was divided up into
two bedrooms with a false ceiling concealing

the plasterwork above; today, the room is
once again the principal entertaining space
in the house and is used for concerts and
recitals.

John Prideaux's descendants did
little to alter the house over the next
one hundred years. Despite the family's
backing of the Parliamentarians during
the English Civil War, a judicious marriage
by Edmund Prideaux's sister Elizabeth to
Sir William Morice, secretary of state to
Charles II, secured a pardon for the family
misdemeanours. It was not until the tenure of
Edmund Prideaux, who inherited the house
in 1728 from his first cousin, that substantial
changes were made to the fabric of the
building. The son of the celebrated scholar
and churchman Humphrey Prideaux, Dean
of Norwich, Edmund was well educated and
went on his Grand Tour in 1739–40. When
that waspish man of letters Horace Walpole

PRECEDING PAGES: *The ceiling of the great chamber was hidden in the eighteenth century, when the room was converted into two bedrooms. Peter Prideaux-Brune remembers crawling along the rafters as a boy and rediscovering it.*

ABOVE: *An early-eighteenth-century view of Prideaux Place overlooking the harbour town of Padstow.*

RIGHT: *A watercolour by Edmund Prideaux showing the remodeled east front, formal gardens, temple, and obelisk that he created in the 1730s.*

OPPOSITE: *Two of Edmund Prideaux's watercolour books, one open at an architectural elevation of the east front. His account book for his Grand Tour (1739–40) lies open above them.*

met him in 1742, he wrote complaining of having been "plagued all morning with that oaf of an unlicked antiquity, Prideaux, and his great boy." Edmund was a talented amateur draftsman, and a series of line and wash drawings he made suggest modifications to the south front. On the entrance front the pointed gables were truncated and given the crenellated profile seen today. He added monuments to the grounds, including the Temple, Obelisk, and Grotto. Inside, he installed some beautifully carved 1680s paneling from Stowe, the Cornish home of Sir Richard Grenville, first Earl of Bath. What had been Grenville's dining room was removed lock, stock, and barrel and

shipped by sea to Prideaux Place, complete with superb gilded carving framing the doors and windows and three paintings by Antonio Verrio. At one end is a stunning oval pier glass composed of crossed palm branches below winged figures with a putti flying above holding garlands of flowers. Restoration portraits hang on the walls, including one of John Wilmot, the "Wicked" Earl of Rochester, famous as a poet and wit in Charles II's court. To this day, the room is known as the Grenville Room.

Edmund's son Humphrey duly inherited when his father died in 1745. While he was on his Grand Tour, Venetian painter Rosalba Carriera drew his portrait in pastel. When the picture was cleaned in 1914, a letter proclaiming her love for him was discovered hidden behind it; Humphrey never knew how she really felt about him. Humphrey probably contributed to some of the changes to the grounds, including the Gothic dairy. His son the Reverend Charles Prideaux inherited a sizable fortune from his mother's family, the Brunes, and added Brune to his surname in 1797. The inheritance enabled him to make further alterations to the house, including a fashionable Gothic makeover for the south front and a series of Gothic rooms inside, possibly echoing and alluding to earlier monastic buildings that most likely once stood on the site. At the center of the house he introduced a grand hall with a sweeping staircase; tall Gothic statue niches with intricate canopies grace the walls, and the ceiling is decorated with panels of quatrefoils to give the impression of a vault. A Gothic archway rising over the first landing frames another flight of steps leading to the library; with its ribbed, Gothic-vaulted ceiling and stained-glass window imparting an atmospheric "gloomth," the architecture of the library recalls Horace Walpole's famous Strawberry Hill. The many heiresses who

have married into the family are recalled through the riot of heraldry in the stained-glass windows, and the shelves are stacked two books deep with a collection of over six thousand volumes. The drawing room was placed in the middle of the south front, its bow window filling the space with light. Recently redecorated, this delightful room has a delicate Gothic plasterwork frieze and windows with Gothic detailing. The family shield and crests of a Saracen's head (for Prideaux) and a goat (for Brune) are carved onto the chimneypiece—just one of the many places they appear in the house. Charles Prideaux-Brune also added the Gothic stables, with a charming line of quatrefoil window openings piercing the façade.

Following Charles's death in 1833, very little was done to alter Prideaux Place.

It passed from father to son through the next five generations, and at the turn of the twentieth century became the first house in Cornwall to have its own electricity. During World War II it played host to the American Army, which requisitioned the house. Of its forty-four bedrooms, only six are habitable; the remainder are just as the American Army left them at the end of the war.

In 1988 Peter Prideaux-Brune inherited the house from his father, John, and with his wife, Elisabeth, began an extensive restoration program that continues to the present day. In the grounds, they have restored the Ionic Temple and the Dairy, and, with help from the Cornwall Gardens Trust, re-created the nineteenth-century formal gardens, which were completely overgrown. Peter's childhood teddy bear "Me Too" has become something of a country house celebrity, even having a children's book written about him. True to his name, he appears in the portrait of Peter by Andrew Festing that hangs above the mantelpiece in the library, which is usually where he is found sitting.

PRIDEAUX PLACE

The Breakfast hour is 9.15,
One the hour for Luncheon,
The Post departs Four Forty-five,
Sharp Eight the Dinner function.

Prideaux Place has become a much sought-after location for filmmakers, including dramatizations of Cornwall native Rosamunde Pilcher's novels and an acclaimed production of *Twelfth Night*. Tradition is kept alive through the annual May Day "Obby Oss" (literally, hobby horse) festivities. Taking place starting in the town of Padstow, this ancient May Day event centers around the "Blue Ribbon Obby Oss" and "Old Obby Oss," who dance through the streets with the people of the town and visit the squire at Prideaux Place. Such a vivid example of a centuries-old tradition, whose origins are lost in the mists of time, would be hard to find, and it seems to sit happily with the great house overlooking the town and the sea beyond.

PRECEDING PAGES LEFT: *A Regency metamorphic table in the library converts into a ladder.*

PRECEDING PAGES RIGHT, CLOCKWISE FROM TOP: *The drawing room; in days gone by, guests were informed of the daily timetable by a card left in their bedroom; a bedroom overlooking the gardens.*

ABOVE: *Looking out over the mock battlements toward the deer park.*

RIGHT: *The south front, glimpsed from the drive.*

OPPOSITE TOP: *Sunrise over the deer park.*

OPPOSITE BOTTOM: *The entrance front of Prideaux Place with its crenellated profile and curtain wall.*

In 1917, while the house was being used as a convalescent home for British Army officers, the ten-year-old Daphne du Maurier made the first of several visits to Milton. Years later, when she was writing Rebecca, she based the interiors of Manderley on her childhood memories of Milton.

The Fitzwilliams of Milton were once one of the most powerful families in the country. They descend from a junior branch of the medieval Fitzwilliams of Sprotborough in Yorkshire and first came to Milton in 1502, when Sir William Fitzwilliam bought the manor from Robert Whittelbury, whose family had owned it since 1391. Like so many of the builders of great houses in this part of the world, Sir William's fortune was based on the wool trade. He was treasurer to Cardinal Wolsey, Henry VIII's famous Lord Chancellor, and entertained the disgraced cleric at

Milton in 1530, much to Henry's annoyance. However, when Sir William explained that he had done so not from any disloyalty to his Sovereign but from a sense of gratitude to Wolsey, all was forgiven. In 1620 the family was raised to the peerage and, through the marriage of the third Earl Fitzwilliam to Lady Anne Watson-Wentworth in 1744, eventually came to inherit the vast Yorkshire estates that her brother, the celebrated Whig Prime Minister, the second Marquess of Rockingham, left to her son, the fourth Earl Fitzwilliam. At this point, Milton ceased to

PRECEDING PAGES: *The North Hall was remodeled by Henry Flitcroft in 1750; a wind dial and map of Europe are incorporated into the overmantel. A full-length portrait of the Duke of Buckingham hangs at one end.*

OPPOSITE: *The bay window in the North Hall dates from the mid-sixteenth century. The coat of arms of the Earls Fitzwilliam appears in the stained glass and the park can be glimpsed beyond.*

LEFT: *A drawing dated 1721 shows the house before the roof was raised (to provide accommodation for servants) in 1771 under the direction of architect Sir William Chambers.*

THE OLD FRONT OF THE EARL FITZWILLIAM'S HOUSE AT MILTON, AUG. 2 1721

RIGHT: *The portrait of
James I that was given by
Mary, Queen of Scots to
Sir William Fitzwilliam III
on the morning of her
execution.*

OPPOSITE: *A lead statue of
a classical figure stands in
front of the stables.*

OVERLEAF: *The stable
court, designed by William
Talman in 1690, can be
glimpsed behind a row of
pleached lime trees. The
bay window of the North
Hall is on the far right.*

be the principal seat and was replaced by the
palatial Wentworth Woodhouse. As a happy
result, Milton was spared any insensitive
Victorian makeovers; its earlier building
history, however, is somewhat complicated.

There must have been a manor house
of some note at Milton for Sir William
Fitzwilliam to entertain his erstwhile
employer Cardinal Wolsey; but that a tent
had to be erected for the occasion suggests
that the house was not huge. The earliest part
of the house is probably the area containing
the North Hall, which protrudes slightly
on the north front. Its 17-degree difference
in alignment from the rest of the front may
represent the footprint of part of the building
that Sir William bought in 1502. Indeed, its
layout is typical of a medieval great hall. It is
lit by a magnificent four-tiered bay window
with stone mullions framing heraldic stained
glass; the rounded, arched mullions date
from about 1540–50. A rough plan dated 1582
shows the house with only two oriels near
each other, so the matching bay window
that now stands at the west extremity of
the north front may have been moved there

when the other five oriels were added; these
have square-headed mullions dating from
about 1600. Sir William, who died in 1534,
may have been responsible for the mid-
sixteenth-century works at the end of his
life, but they may have been overseen by his
son Sir William Fitzwilliam II. His grandson
Sir William Fitzwilliam III served twice as
Lord Deputy of Ireland for Elizabeth I. As
Constable of Fotheringhay Castle, he had the
unpleasant duty of supervising the trial and
execution of Mary, Queen of Scots. Family
tradition holds that on the morning of her
execution she gave Sir William a treasured
portrait of her son, James I, as a boy in
appreciation for his kindness and sympathy.
The little painting still remains at Milton.
Sir William III was probably responsible
for much of the building of the north front,
adding the five oriels, which together with
the classical porch, give the north front a
rhythmical and stately quality, stretching
as it does over 235 feet.

The north front was made even longer
by the addition of the three-sided stable
court on the east end in 1690 by the first
Earl Fitzwilliam. The architect was William
Talman, Comptroller of the King's Works and
the architect of Chatsworth in Derbyshire.
He was probably chosen because he was a
pupil of the first earl's renowned brother-
in-law, Sir Christopher Wren. With its
pedimented central bays topped by a cupola
and embracing flanking wings, the stable
court is a dignified composition suitable for
a nobleman who was made Viscount Milton
and Earl Fitzwilliam in 1716. More stables
were added in 1720 by his son the second earl
a year after he inherited Milton.

Milton is a house of surprises, and
nothing quite prepares the visitor for the
change in style from the Elizabethan north
front, where one enters, to the Palladian
south front. Like Felbrigg Hall in Norfolk

OPPOSITE TOP:
The Elizabethan north front and Talman stable court seen from the park.

OPPOSITE BOTTOM:
The Palladian south front, designed by Henry Flitcroft. The shallow, two-storey bow window on the far right was added by John Carr of York in 1792.

TOP LEFT: *The pillared hall occupies the center of the ground floor on the south front. The painted decoration from the 1950s has been carefully preserved.*

BOTTOM LEFT: *The main staircase features superb stucco decoration by Thomas Clark, carried out in the mid-eighteenth century, and a graceful balustrade of gilt and wrought-iron scrolled leaves.*

and Stapleford Park in Leicestershire, the two styles seem to cohabit quite happily, although it was clearly a challenge to incorporate the old into the new. Talman (in 1688), James Gibbs (in 1726), and Matthew Brettingham (in 1749) all put forward proposals for modernizing or rebuilding the old house, but these came to naught. It was left to the third earl to initiate the works and he employed Henry Flitcroft in 1749.

The choice was a natural one; the third earl's marriage to Lady Anne Watson-Wentworth must have brought him into contact with Flitcroft, who was enlarging her father's great seat, Wentworth Woodhouse. For Milton, Flitcroft designed an entirely new south front, sweeping away the two old ranges that had extended from the house at right angles. Although long, Flitcroft's south façade is relieved by a pedimented central bay with a Venetian window on the middle floor below a Diocletian window. Each end has a short projecting wing with canted bay windows. Inside, the central five bays of the ground floor are occupied by a pillared hall that connects to the old North Hall at the main staircase, a beautiful top-lit space with stucco decoration by the London craftsman

Thomas Clark. The stairs are embellished by a graceful balustrade composed of richly scrolled leaves in gilt and wrought iron, similar to one at Holkham Hall in Norfolk. Flitcroft gave the North Hall a deep, coved ceiling and a boldly carved chimneypiece (by John Deval, Sr.) incorporating a wind dial on a map of Europe. This is an imposing room,

with "azalea pink" walls, supposedly the colour given them by Flitcroft and carefully repainted in the 1950s. Three Kentian painted tables with marble tops stand against the walls beneath full-length portraits, including one of the notorious Duke of Buckingham, James I's favourite. Upstairs, one of Flitcroft's bedrooms is papered with Chinese paintings framed in fret-patterned strips to give the effect of wallpaper. Another of Flitcroft's bedrooms, featuring a boldly carved chimneypiece and overmantel, contains a fine mahogany four-post bed of about 1760 with its original pierced and painted cresting and chintz hangings.

Tragically, the third Earl Fitzwilliam died at the age of only thirty-seven in 1756, so Flitcroft's work was never completed. It was left to his son the fourth earl to finish the house, and this he did shortly after he came of age in 1770. He commissioned Sir William Chambers, architect to George III, who had just completed the Palladian villa Roehampton in Surrey for his father-in-law, the second Earl of Bessborough. Chambers added a new dining room (now the Smoking Room) on the ground floor of the north front and the Peterborough Dining Room, Tea Room, and Green Library on the first floor of the north front. The Peterborough Dining Room has a fine neoclassical ceiling and is now used as a drawing room, hung with two sensational portraits by Sir Joshua Reynolds. Chambers's most splendid addition was the Gallery, which dominates the first and second floors of the south front and is one of the great surprises at Milton. The spectacular plasterwork ceiling is divided into three parts: a shallow central dome flanked by barrel vaults. On the exterior, Chambers ingeniously raised the roof on the north front to provide bedrooms for servants, the dormer windows being built mainly in wood to lessen the weight, but painted to imitate

stone. Likewise, the use of the French-style mansard roof produced the necessary height without the need for building another storey.

The final stage of building came in 1792, when John Carr of York designed a large and a small library with a broad and shallow two-storey bow window on the south front. Carr had been employed earlier by the fourth earl at Wentworth Woodhouse, which he had inherited in 1782 on the death of his uncle, the second Marquess of Rockingham. The landscape architect Humphry Repton was also employed in the 1790s, and he produced one of his famous Red Books (handwritten and illustrated proposals for landscape designs, named for their red morocco bindings) for Milton.

After the death of the fourth Earl Fitzwilliam in 1833, Milton passed to his only son, the fifth earl, and was mainly used in the winter for the fox hunting, where the Fitzwilliam hounds were (and still are) kenneled. The fifth earl in turn left Milton to his younger son, George Wentworth-Fitzwilliam, while the main branch of the family continued to reside at Wentworth Woodhouse. In 1917, while the house was being used as a convalescent home for British Army officers, the ten year-old Daphne du Maurier made the first of

several visits to Milton. Years later, when she was writing *Rebecca*, she based the interiors of Manderley on her childhood memories of Milton.

In 1948, Peter, the eighth Earl Fitzwilliam, was killed in a plane crash with his lover, Kathleen "Kick" Kennedy, sister of J.F.K. (she had been widowed herself during World War II when her husband, Billy, Marquess of Hartington was killed in action). The Fitzwilliam title briefly passed to a cousin, Eric, until he died in 1952. It then went to a second cousin, Captain Tom Fitzwilliam, and once again Milton was united with the title. Today, Milton is the home of the tenth earl's grandson, Sir Philip Naylor-Leyland, Bt., who inherited it from his mother. He and his family maintain the house and estate to the highest standards, in a way that would make his ancestors proud.

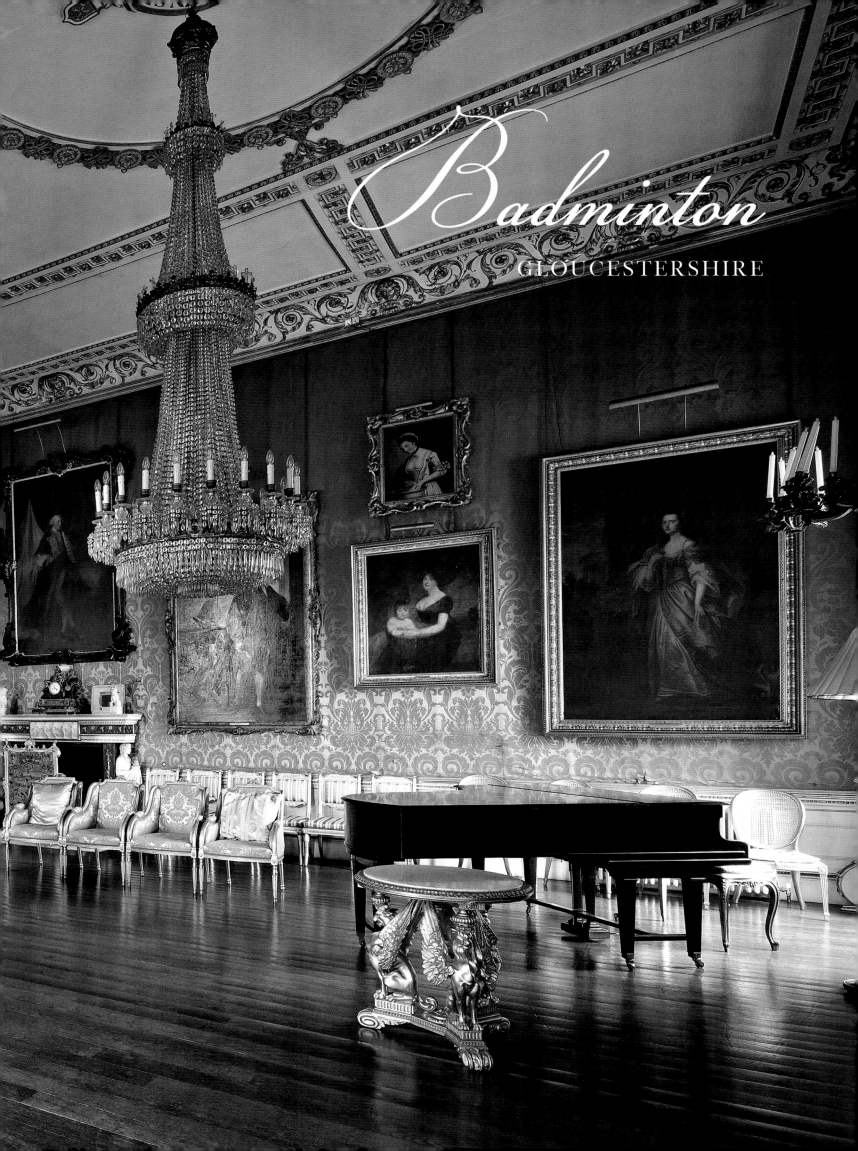

Badminton

GLOUCESTERSHIRE

uring World War II, Queen Mary descended on Badminton and stayed there throughout the war as a guest of her niece the Duchess of Beaufort. When the Queen arrived, the duchess looked on with horror as the Queen's seventy pieces of personal luggage were unloaded by a retinue of fifty-five servants; three suitcases were always kept packed in case she needed to escape should the Nazis attempt to kidnap her.

The magnificent Worcester Lodge, a masterpiece of Palladian architecture by William Kent, crowns the horizon as one approaches Badminton from the north. Then, at the end of the three-mile Great Avenue, the house looms into view, its twin domes glinting beneath the fluttering flag of the Duke of Beaufort. The grandeur of the house and the vast expanse of wooded

PRECEDING PAGES: *Jeffry Wyatville created the Great Drawing Room for the sixth Duke of Beaufort in 1811–12 out of what was previously the library. The plasterwork ceiling by Francis Bernasconi incorporates the Order of the Garter.*

OPPOSITE: *Badminton boasts a fine collection of family portraits; those in the East Room are here reflected in the Palladian overmantel mirror with its sunburst frame.*

TOP LEFT: *Bell pulls at the end of the long corridor leading to the octagonal Waiting Room.*

BOTTOM LEFT: *A view of the north front of Badminton, painted for the second Duke of Beaufort about 1710, showing the great rides radiating out from the house into the surrounding landscape.*

ABOVE LEFT: *The seventh Duke of Beaufort in his Garter robes by Franz Xaver Winterhalter.*

ABOVE RIGHT: *The tenth Duke of Beaufort, known as "Master," painted in his Garter robes by Sir Oswald Birley.*

OPPOSITE TOP: *Worcester Lodge, designed by William Kent, stands at the beginning of the three-mile Great Avenue.*

OPPOSITE BOTTOM: *The view down the Great Avenue from Worcester Lodge, with the house just visible in the distance.*

OVERLEAF: *The north front seen from the park. William Kent added the wooden cupolas and pediment in the mid-eighteenth century.*

parkland surrounding it make one feel like one has entered a princely kingdom. Indeed, the Dukes of Beaufort are descended from Edward III's son John of Gaunt; hence the appearance of the quartered arms of England and France on the flag.

Badminton is recorded in the Domesday Book as "Madmintune" and was owned by the Boteler family from 1275 to 1612, when Thomas Somerset, fourth Earl of Worcester, purchased the manors of Great and Little Badminton. Five years later, he gave Badminton to his third son, Sir Thomas Somerset, as a wedding present, and Sir Thomas proceeded to modernize the old Boteler residence. The subsequent architectural history of Badminton is far from straightforward. Like a courtier, the house has changed its formal attire according to the prevailing fashions of the day. Sir Thomas incorporated much of the Boteler

house in his alterations. His great nephew Henry Somerset, first Duke of Beaufort, upgraded the house in keeping with his new status. The work began in 1664 and was not finished until 1691. The north front was modeled on Queen Henrietta Maria's New Gallery at Somerset House by John Webb and forms the core of the present north façade. It is juxtaposed with the lower, pedimented, and hipped-roofed east front—visible in an engraving of about 1669—which looked out over the privy gardens, parterres, and hornbeam wilderness laid out by the Duchess of Beaufort, a celebrated horticulturalist. Her husband's grandiose schemes transformed the park beyond, with thirty rides radiating out from the house.

The first duke was succeeded by a grandson who employed a local Bath architect, William Killigrew, to make further alterations. The west front is largely

OPPOSITE: *The octagonal Waiting Room was decorated in the rococo style by Thomas Paty in 1750.*

FAR LEFT: *A musical trophy, executed in plasterwork, over the mantelpiece in the Waiting Room.*

LEFT: *Nineteenth-century battledores (rackets) and shuttlecocks; the modern game of badminton was invented in the Great Hall at Badminton.*

OVERLEAF: *The Great Hall has a series of five equestrian and hunting paintings by John Wootton. The life-size horse over the mantelpiece is Grey Barb, a famous Arabian stallion belonging to the third Duke of Beaufort.*

Killigrew's work of about 1708; when viewed from across the pond, it is flanked by single-storey pavilions, one built as a brew house, the other as a laundry and now the home of John Harris, the eminent architectural historian who has done much to unravel the complex building history of Badminton. Killigrew also tinkered with the fenestration on the north front and designed most of the ochre-colored estate houses in the village.

Further enhancements to the house were made by the third Duke of Beaufort, who succeeded his father in 1714, when he was only seven. His Grand Tour in the 1720s fired an interest in architecture that led to his employing Francis Smith of Warwick on his return. Smith added an attic floor and pediment to the east front, thereby bringing it into unison with the north front, but losing its balance in the process. His chief legacy is the decoration of the Great Hall, which, like that of the rest of the house, is far from clear-cut. Edward Poynton carved the Corinthian pillars and door cases, while

Charles Stanley and Thomas Roberts were paid for plasterwork in 1739 and 1753, respectively. John Morley was paid for the plasterwork ceiling in 1751. Ranged around the room are five great hunting canvases by the celebrated equestrian painter John Wootton; a recent discovery has revealed that two are signed and dated 1732. The second pair was painted twelve years later, and over the chimneypiece is a life-size study of the duke's famous Arabian stallion, Grey Barb (1734). All have superb gilded frames, probably by John Boson. It was in this room that the foundations of the modern game of badminton were laid, an adaptation of a game played in British India, particularly in the garrison town of Poona (now Pune). Two battledores (rackets) survive, both inscribed by Lady Henrietta Somerset, daughter of the seventh duke, and dated January 12, 1830, and February 1845, respectively. The standard size of a badminton court is that of the Great Hall.

Opening off the Great Hall is an octagonal anteroom known as the Waiting

ABOVE: *Superb carving by Grinling Gibbons hangs over the mantelpiece in the Great Dining Room, flanked by portraits of the fourth Duke and Duchess of Beaufort.*

OPPOSITE, CLOCKWISE FROM TOP LEFT: *The interior of the church looking toward the family balcony at the west end; the first Duke of Beaufort's monument, by Grinling Gibbons; the fourth duke's monument, by John Michael Rysbrack; the second and third dukes' monument, also by Rysbrack.*

Room, decorated by Thomas Paty in 1750. Its delicate rococo plasterwork includes a musical trophy over the mantelpiece and an Apollo mask and sunburst on the ceiling. Nearby is the baroque Great Dining Room designed by Smith. It houses the celebrated Grinling Gibbons limewood carvings, executed in 1683–84 for Beaufort House, Chelsea, and brought to Badminton in 1717–18. Full-length ducal family portraits by Kneller, Dahl, Hudson, and Smirke dominate the walls between Corinthian pilasters.

Smith died in 1738, and James Gibbs succeeded him as architect. He added pedimented pavilions at each end of the north front, but with the third duke's death in 1746, yet another architect, the famous William Kent, was brought in. Kent designed the great two-tier pediment crowning the north front and its flanking cupolas, all constructed from wood painted to look like stone (for lightness).

His other work on the north front included adding giant rusticated pilasters to the Gibbs pavilions, echoed in those flanking the front door.

The fifth duke rebuilt the old church between 1782 and 1785 to designs by Charles Evans. More akin to a London city church than a country chapel, it houses Grinling Gibbons's huge monument to the first duke (removed from the Somerset Chapel in St. George's Chapel, Windsor Castle, at the behest of Queen Victoria) and John Michael Rysbrack's two monuments, one for the second and third dukes (1754), the other for the fourth duke (1756).

Badminton was further aggrandized by the sixth Duke of Beaufort, who employed Jeffry Wyatville, from the famous Wyatt dynasty of architects, in 1809–13. Wyatville's main alteration was the creation of the Great Drawing Room, with its Order of

the Garter–themed plasterwork ceiling and magnificent neoclassical Italian chimneypiece, designed by James Byres for the Dowager Duchess of Beaufort, widow of the fourth duke, in 1773. The ormolu mounts are by Luigi Valadier and on each side stands a vestal virgin. Wyatville moved the bookcases that had formerly lined the room to their present location in the Library, where two views of Badminton by Canaletto have pride of place: one looks out to the Great Lawn, complete with follies and park buildings; the other looks back to the house as left by Kent. Wyatville also rebuilt the staircase; its ramps seem to rise up in all directions through the center of the house. Here and elsewhere the walls are lined with family portraits—nearly two hundred in all. Some of the earliest portraits are hung in the Family Dining Room, which has striking yellow arabesque wallpaper designed by

Thomas Willement, who supplied stained glass to the church in the mid-nineteenth century. Two other rooms on the east front are also hung with Willement wallpaper: the East Room (hung with late–seventeenth- and early-eighteenth-century portraits) and the Duchess's Sitting Room. The latter has a charming portrait of the fifth duke as a boy with his tutor by Sir Joshua Reynolds.

Outside, the gardens and park have undergone similar reincarnations over the centuries. The present duke employed François Goffinet to design a formal, compartmented garden in 1990, incorporating a shell garden created by his duchess. There are many notable buildings peppering the estate, including Swangrove, which was built as a hunting lodge for Sir Thomas Somerset and remodeled for the second duke by Killigrew in 1703. Thomas Wright, the "Wizard of Durham" and a friend of the fourth duke and his "bluestocking" duchess, Elizabeth Berkeley, designed several quirky buildings on the estate.

During World War II, Queen Mary descended on Badminton and stayed there throughout the war as a guest of her niece the Duchess of Beaufort. When the Queen arrived, the duchess looked on with horror as the Queen's seventy pieces of personal luggage were unloaded by a retinue of fifty-five servants; three suitcases were always kept packed in case she needed to escape should the Nazis attempt to kidnap her.

Today, Badminton is probably best known for the annual Horse Trials, which take place in early May. Started in 1949 by the tenth Duke of Beaufort, they are the equestrian equivalent of Wimbledon or Henley Royal

Regatta. The tenth duke was universally known as "Master," having been given a pack of harriers for his eleventh birthday. He was probably the most renowned Master of Foxhounds of his day and continued a long tradition of hunting dukes; hounds have been kenneled at Badminton since 1640. His grandfather was known as "The Blue Duke" after the colours of the Beaufort Hunt. He was one of the best-known sporting figures in England and edited the *Badminton Library of Sports and Pastimes,* a collection of books covering everything from archery to figure skating.

The current Duke of Beaufort is chairman of Marlborough Fine Art (London) Ltd., one of the world's leading contemporary art dealerships. Thanks to his assured eye and natural style, Badminton has been lovingly restored and is to many people the epitome of the English country house.

OPPOSITE: *The previous Duchess of Beaufort's bedroom is hung with several fine pastel portraits.*

ABOVE: *The Chinese Bedroom; the bed is a copy of the original by William and John Linnell, now in the Victoria and Albert Museum.*

LEFT: *Detail of the Chinese Export wallpaper.*

OVERLEAF LEFT, CLOCKWISE FROM TOP LEFT: *The view through Clock Arch down the drive; an eighteenth-century door by Francis Smith; the east front.*

OVERLEAF RIGHT: *The church overlooking the formal garden, laid out for the present duke by François Goffinet.*

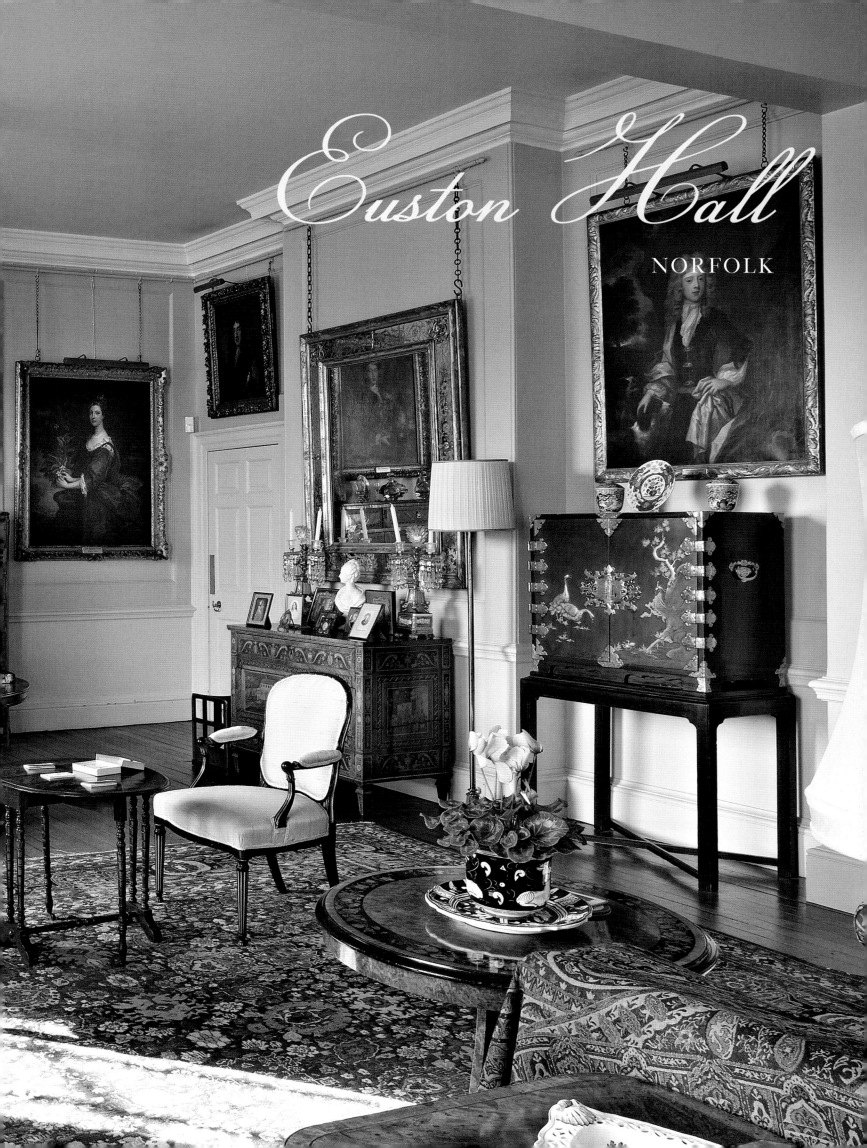

Euston Hall

NORFOLK

*T*he second Duke of Grafton was succeeded by his grandson
Augustus, who served as prime minister from 1768 to 1770.
Portraits of the second and third dukes by such eighteenth-century
luminaries as Sir Joshua Reynolds and Pompeo Batoni grace the
walls at Euston and join a staggering array of seventeenth-century
portraits, many depicting members of the royal family.

Euston, lying on the border between Suffolk and Norfolk, still echoes with the sounds of Charles II's court. John Evelyn, the famous diarist and gardener, gives us a vivid picture of the house "fill'd from one end to the other with lords, ladys and gallants," all guests of the Earl of Arlington, Charles II's Secretary of State and later Lord Chamberlain. It was during a house party in 1671 that the King, who had traveled over from his palace at Newmarket, finally had his wicked way

with Louise de Keroualle, thus spawning the Richmond dynasty, whose seat at Goodwood is described in another chapter.

Arlington had purchased the run-down estate in 1666. Its origins can be traced back to the Domesday Book, when it was in ecclesiastical ownership. It later passed into the hands of the Rookwood family, with whom Queen Elizabeth I stayed in the summer of 1578, on her way to Norwich. Arlington decided to build a new house

PRECEDING PAGES: *The drawing room is hung with a fine collection of family portraits, including one of the third Duke of Grafton, seen above the open door to the inner hall.*

OPPOSITE: *Van Dyck's portrait of Charles I is reflected in a gilt-wood mirror in the outer hall.*

LEFT: *The inner hall; van Dyck's portrait of Thomas Wentworth, first Earl of Strafford, hangs in the left archway. He was impeached by Parliament in 1641 and later executed.*

Canall at Euston and orangerie

Back front of Euston & Orangerie towards ye West.

foundation stone in 1676 and it was quickly finished the following year. Evelyn described it as "one of the prettiest in England."

Evelyn advised Arlington on the landscaping of the gardens and park, much of which survives to this day. Great avenues planted to the east and the west link the house with the surrounding landscape, as Arlington had obtained a royal license to impark 2,000 acres in Euston and the adjoining parishes. Evelyn ordered "plantations of firs, elms, limes &c. up his parke, and in all other places and avenues." A drawing by Edmund Prideaux shows the west front with an orangery, a formal garden, and a canal in about 1716.

Lord and Lady Arlington had only one child, a beloved daughter, Isabella. At the tender age of five, she was betrothed to Henry FitzRoy, the nine-year-old son of Charles II by his mistress the Duchess of Cleveland. They were remarried seven years later, by which time Henry had been created Duke of Grafton. A grand baroque portrait of the first Duke of Grafton by Thomas Hawker shows a dark and handsome young man standing proudly in his Garter robes. He was a brave soldier and sailor who fought two duels and later joined Prince William of Orange when he landed in England. Sadly, he lost his life fighting for the prince at the siege of Cork in 1690, aged only twenty-seven. His young widow was painted two years later with the second duke, aged nine, by Sir Godfrey Kneller.

Later in life, the second Duke of Grafton, who was passionate about hunting and horseracing, turned to more aesthetic pursuits and decided to remodel his grandfather's house and update the grounds. He was introduced to William Kent, probably by the Earl of Burlington, who had built a wooden bridge over what had been the canal but now meandered in an irregular

in the French manner, with three wings around a central court and a square pavilion surmounted by a dome at each corner. A painting by Thomas Wyck shows the new house, finished in 1670, with flags fluttering atop each dome and a stag hunt taking place in the foreground. Evelyn described it as "very magnificent and commodious, as well within as without, nor lesse splendidly furnish'd." The renowned Italian baroque painter Antonio Verrio executed superb ceiling paintings; Arlington was one of Verrio's first patrons in England. In the grounds of his new mansion, Arlington rebuilt the parish church, which is visible in the Wyck painting. His daughter laid the

manner. Not long ago, two sketches by Kent were discovered rolled up at the back of a drawer, one a design for a new grand, pedimented house with flanking wings and pavilions, the other showing the view westward from the proposed house and featuring a pedimented arch and flanking lodges on the horizon. Although the proposed house was never built, the arch and lodges were, and still are, a focal point up the hill to the west, where a lime avenue, known as "Duke's Ride," extends for several miles beyond. Kent's sketch of the proposed house also shows a domed banqueting house, known as the Temple, on the horizon. This exquisite building was executed, although it was sited farther to the south and must have been an excellent place for the duke to watch his racehorses exercising or the hunt in progress. When Kent died in 1748, the duke was nearly seventy, and he decided to rebuild

his grandfather's house rather than tear it down and build on a new site. His architect for the project was the talented Matthew Brettingham, who had overseen the building of Holkham Hall to Kent and Burlington's designs. Brettingham refaced the house in red brick with stone dressings, refenestrated it, and added pediments to the south and east fronts. The domed pavilions were replaced by square turrets with pyramidal roofs similar to those at Holkham. He deepened the north front, adding a new façade with a porch and a rusticated doorway. It is crowned by a long balustrade that is relieved by the twin pavilions rising behind. This façade formed an alternative entrance to the house, approached through a rusticated archway in the stables that leads into a courtyard. The courtyard façade of the stables was also given a face-lift: a central pediment below a cupola flanked by segmental arch windows on the ground floor and square sash windows above.

The second Duke of Grafton was succeeded by his grandson Augustus, who served as prime minister from 1768 to 1770. Portraits of the second and third dukes by such eighteenth-century luminaries as Sir Joshua Reynolds and Pompeo Batoni grace the walls at Euston and join a staggering

OPPOSITE: *A portrait of Henry, first Duke of Grafton by Thomas Hawker hangs in the dining room. He was the illegitimate son of Charles II by Barbara Villiers, Duchess of Cleveland and was killed at the siege of Cork at only twenty-seven years of age.*

TOP LEFT: *Isabella, wife of the first Duke of Grafton, with their son, the second duke, painted by Sir Godfrey Kneller. She inherited Euston from her father, Lord Arlington.*

BOTTOM LEFT: *Augustus, third Duke of Grafton by Pompeo Batoni. He was prime minister from 1768 to 1770.*

OVERLEAF: *The south front seen from across the lawns.*

array of seventeenth-century portraits, many depicting members of the royal family. The entrance hall is dominated by a superb painting of Charles I standing elegantly beside a grey horse pawing the ground by Sir Anthony van Dyck. Nearby is a portrait of the king's five eldest children, also by van Dyck, flanked by busts of Charles I and Charles II. The dining room, which is the largest room in the house, has portraits of a youthful Charles II (by Philippe de Champaigne), his brother, James II (by Lely), his youngest sister, Henrietta, Duchess of Orleans (by Mignard), his mother, Queen Henrietta Maria (by van Dyck), and his grandparents James I and Anne of Denmark (by van Somer). A full-length portrait by Lely of Lord Arlington depicts him in his robes as a Knight of the Garter; over his nose he wears a black plaster that covered the scar of a sabre cut he received during the Civil War.

Tragically, fire destroyed the west and south wings in 1902 together with their fine Verrio ceilings, though most of the contents were saved. The wings were rebuilt in the same form externally, but by 1952 the house was too big for post–World War II living, so the tenth duke took down the rebuilt wings, leaving only the north range and the stables. As a result, the house may have a slightly truncated appearance on the garden front, but the approach through the archway into the north court was preserved and the sun streams through the south-facing windows. The drawing room lies on this front and is formed from two smaller rooms. Painted a duck-egg blue and filled with natural light, it is hung with some of the eighteenth-century family portraits, including Batoni's portrait of the third duke on his Grand Tour. Van Dyck's double portrait of Charles I and Henrietta Maria is displayed over the mantelpiece.

The late (eleventh) Duke of Grafton was a champion of England's heritage and conservation. It is therefore entirely appropriate that among the many projects he carried out at Euston was the restoration of the King Charles gates and the long stretch

of railings that had been built by his ancestor Lord Arlington to impress his royal visitor Charles II. They were rededicated by Her Majesty The Queen Mother in 1994. The Dowager Duchess of Grafton has been Mistress of the Robes to Her Majesty The Queen since 1967 and lived at Euston until 2011, when her grandson succeeded as duke.

OPPOSITE: *Looking down the nave of the church at Euston, which is more like a City of London church than a country church.*

ABOVE: *The church seen from the park.*

LEFT: *Matthew Brettingham's north front engraved on a glass bowl that was presented to the eleventh Duke of Grafton.*

Goodwood House

SUSSEX

Today, Goodwood is celebrated as England's greatest sporting estate. It is the first estate on which cricket was regularly played. . . . In addition to the horse racing, there is golf, flying, and motor sport. The last brings hundreds of thousands of spectators to the annual Festival of Speed, staged in the park, and the Goodwood Revival, which takes place at the Motor Circuit.

Goodwood lies at the foot of the South Downs, its three façades with copper-domed turrets looking out across a well-wooded park where sheep safely graze. It has been the seat of the Dukes of Richmond since the late seventeenth century, when the first Duke of Richmond, an illegitimate son of Charles II by his French mistress Louise de Keroualle, came here to enjoy the fox hunting in the nearby village of Charlton. The Charlton Hunt attracted the cream of English society, including the duke's elder half-brother, the ill-fated Duke of Monmouth, another natural son of Charles II.

Little remains of the original hunting lodge that the young Duke of Richmond rented and later bought in 1697. It had been built in the second decade of the seventeenth century by the "Wizard" Earl of Northumberland from nearby Petworth, and gabled wings had subsequently been added. Sash windows soon graced the front of the house and it was given a classical makeover when the second Duke of Richmond employed the architect Roger Morris to

remodel the Jacobean hall (known as the Long Hall) in 1730. Screens of columns and a pair of Palladian chimneypieces were added to form a suitable space for hunt breakfasts, as the duke had become Master of the Charlton Hunt that same year.

The second duke was a Renaissance man who had developed a love of classical architecture while on his Grand Tour. The family's principal residence, Richmond House in Whitehall, London, was remodeled by the "Apollo of the Arts," the third Earl of Burlington, and many of the furnishings were almost certainly designed by William Kent. Back at Goodwood, Roger Morris designed a classical banqueting house in the park, its elevated position taking in the far-reaching views to the south coast and the Isle of Wight. It was named Carné's Seat because it replaced a cottage in which Louise de Keroualle's old retainer, Monsieur de Carné, had lived. Nearby, the family helped professional artists decorate a tiny Palladian grotto, known as the Shell House, with hundreds of thousands of shells collected from the South Seas. Not far away, exotic animals, including lions, tigers, bears, monkeys, eagles, and ostriches, filled a menagerie; a stone memorial to a lioness still stands at the top of the garden.

The house was hung with new works of art commissioned by the duke, including six paintings of his horses by leading equestrian painter John Wootton and a pair of magnificent views of London (looking from Richmond House) by Canaletto, designed to hang over the chimneypieces in the Long Hall. The architect Matthew Brettingham was employed by the second duke to extend Goodwood House to the south by building a pedimented façade aligned with the spire of Chichester Cathedral. Alas, the duke died suddenly in 1750, leaving the new wing unfinished and his son still a minor.

The present appearance of Goodwood owes most to the third Duke of Richmond. Like his father, he went on the Grand Tour as a young man, which inspired a love not only of classical art and architecture but also of science (he studied medical science at the University of Leiden). He served in the army, ending up a field marshal, and founded the Royal Ordnance Survey to map the whole of Britain at one inch to the mile. A short posting as ambassador to the Court of Louis XV at Versailles resulted in a gift from the French king of four Gobelins tapestries depicting scenes from Cervantes' *Don Quixote*. On his

OPPOSITE: *In the Long Hall, Henri Gascars's portrait of Charles II depicts Louise de Keroualle in the background; it is the only known picture showing Charles with one of his mistresses. George Stubbs's brooding study of a lioness and two lions hangs beneath it.*

TOP LEFT: *The gateway to Carné's Seat, the second Duke of Richmond's banqueting house, in the park.*

BOTTOM LEFT: *The sixth Duke of Richmond's monogram and the year commemorate the building of the new kennels (in brick and flint) for the Goodwood foxhounds.*

OVERLEAF: *Brettingham's south front catches the sun on a stormy summer's day; a rainbow arcs over Wyatt's entrance front.*

return to Goodwood, the duke commissioned the young James Wyatt to design a room around them and the sculptor John Bacon to carve a beautiful figural chimneypiece. The Paris posting also produced a very important commission of Sèvres porcelain that entailed the factory artists' going to the duke's residence to copy birds from his father's bird books. This was the first time naturalistic birds had been painted on Sèvres ware.

Horses remained a central feature of life at Goodwood in the second half of the eighteenth century. Not long after he came of age, the third duke commissioned Sir William Chambers to design a new stable block, one of Chambers's first commissions outside of London. With its Doric-columned triumphal arch and pristine flintwork, the resulting building was so grand that it outshone the house. In 1801, toward the end of his life, the duke held a private race meeting up in the Downs. It was such a success that the following year he decided to make it a public meeting, and racing has taken place at Goodwood ever since. Even today, the racehorses lodge in the stables.

Building projects at Goodwood kept James Wyatt busy. In addition to the north wing, which included the Tapestry Drawing Room, he designed the Orangery; Molecomb house for the duke's disgraced sister Lady Sarah; the Kennels to house the duke's foxhounds; two lodges for the whippers-in; and the pair of lodges on either side of the road at Pilley Green. Tragically, Richmond House burned down in 1791, although much of the great art collection was saved. The duke's finances were not in good enough shape to rebuild it, so Wyatt designed two new wings to house the art, and work began at the start of the nineteenth century. Designed in the picturesque manner to take advantage of the sweeping views beyond Boxgrove Priory to the sea, the wings were angled away from

the existing house. They included a new entrance hall with a screen of Guernsey granite columns, brought across the English Channel on the duke's yacht. The hall serves as the backdrop for three paintings by George Stubbs of scenes on the estate: *Racehorses Exercising at Goodwood*, *The Charlton Hunt*, and *Shooting at Goodwood*. Stubbs stayed at

Goodwood for nine months in 1759–60, and it was this commission that helped launch his career as one of England's greatest equestrian painters. To the west of the entrance hall is the Egyptian Dining Room with its striking scagliola walls and Egyptian motifs. This room was completely dismantled in the Edwardian era, reputedly because Edward VII did not like it, and was only recently restored. The Yellow Drawing Room is found to the east of the hall; it is hung with eighteenth-century portraits of British monarchs and family members, including three of the handsome third duke (by Mengs, Reynolds, and Romney).

Unfortunately, the third duke died in 1806 before the new wings were completed. His huge debts stalled completion until 1836, when the family coffers were boosted by the great Gordon inheritance (the fifth Duke of Richmond was the nephew of the fifth and last Duke of Gordon, the Gordon clan chieftain known as "Cock of the North"). The fifth duke developed the racecourse, and the annual Raceweek, dubbed "Glorious Goodwood" by the press of the day, became a popular addition to the English social season. The presence of royalty during Raceweek, particularly the Prince of Wales, later Edward VII, increased Goodwood's status dramatically, and the estate became the site of lavish house parties, particularly during the seventh duke's tenure.

Today, Goodwood is celebrated as England's greatest sporting estate. It is the first estate on which cricket was regularly played; the earliest known laws of the game were written in 1727 for a match between the second duke's team and Mr. A. Brodrick's. In addition to the horse racing, there is golf (there is a Championship course and a Public course), flying (the Aerodrome is a former World War II fighter station), and motor sport. The last brings hundreds of thousands of spectators to the annual Festival of Speed, staged in the park, and the Goodwood Revival, which takes place at the Motor Circuit.

Goodwood House is lived in by the present Duke of Richmond's son and heir, the Earl of March and Kinrara, and his family. He and his wife were responsible for the

complete redecoration of the house, including the state rooms, after they moved in in 1994. The family occupy Brettingham's south wing, which includes the Large and Small Libraries. The Large Library is one of the most beautiful rooms in England; its bookcases and ceiling are delicately ornamented with classical figures painted by Charles Reuben Riley. The Small Library is a perfectly appointed gentleman's study, fitted out in the early nineteenth century with a balcony that runs around the room. Standing by a writing table is Napoleon's campaign chair, given by the Duke of Wellington to the fourth duke and duchess as a thank-you for hosting the famous Duchess of Richmond's ball in Brussels just a few days before the Battle of Waterloo. Next door is the private dining room, a circular space in one of the corner turrets, densely hung with pictures bought on the Grand Tour, including two exquisite Venetian scenes by Canaletto painted on copper.

Lord March believes passionately that the family should always live in the house: "Everything we do here is centered around the house and ensures that the family can remain here for generations to come." The estate's stunning setting, magnificent art collection, and prestigious sporting activities all come together to give credence to the traditional epithet "Glorious Goodwood."

OPPOSITE: *The private dining room is hung with paintings collected on the Grand Tour, including two Venetian scenes by Canaletto. A portrait of Louise de Keroualle, mother of the first Duke of Richmond, hangs above the mantelpiece.*

ABOVE: *The Ballroom is used regularly for balls and banquets. Many of the portraits depict members of the royal family.*

FAR LEFT: *Charles II's favourite sister, Henrietta, painted by Sir Peter Lely.*

LEFT: *The first Duke of Richmond by William Wissing; he was made a Knight of the Garter when he was only nine years old.*

Hackthorn Hall

LINCOLNSHIRE

Inside the walled garden is a glasshouse containing what is reputed to be the largest privately owned and second-oldest grapevine in Britain. The "Black Hamburg" vine was planted in 1868 by the head gardener, William Popple, and is the same variety as the Hampton Court vine (planted in 1768). Remarkably, it has been tended by only six gardeners in its life.

The Cracrofts, one of the oldest families in Lincolnshire, trace their descent from Walter de Cracroft, Lord of the Manor of Cracroft in Hogsthorpe, a small village situated near the coast. Walter lived in the early 1200s and his descendants remained at Cracroft Hall until the seventeenth century, when the main line died out. A junior branch of the family thrived, however, and in 1618 John Cracroft inherited the manor of Hackthorn from his uncle Robert Grantham of Dunholme, and Cracrofts have lived there ever since. Over the centuries, they married members of other notable Lincolnshire families, amassing land by inheritance, which resulted in various hyphenations of their surname. Among the well-known characters who appear on the Cracroft family tree are such luminaries as Jane Austen, Sir John Franklin (the famous Arctic explorer), and Alfred, Lord Tennyson.

The present house forms a perfect composition of hall and church in a well-wooded parkland setting complete with lake, such as Jane Austen might have described in one of her novels. The original Elizabethan house appears in a charming watercolor by Edmund Cracroft dated 1792. It is of typical H-shaped form with pretty Dutch-style gables on the entrance front and what appear to be sash windows, which must have been

inserted later. To the right can be seen the stables with a coach-and-pair leaving the scene over a triple-arched bridge.

The same year that Edmund Cracroft painted the old hall, his elder brother John embarked on a new seat for the Cracrofts just west of the church. It was designed by James Lewis, a talented neoclassical architect who published two volumes, entitled *Original Designs in Architecture*, in 1780 and 1797. It is possible that Edmund and John's older

PRECEDING PAGES: *Seen from across the park, Hackthorn Hall and church form a charming composition in the landscape.*

OPPOSITE: *The staircase sweeps around the oval stair hall at the center of the house.*

LEFT: *The staircase is lit from above by a glass dome ornamented with pretty neoclassical plasterwork.*

ELEVATION design'd for the South Front of Hackthorn.

ELEVATION design'd for the North Front of Hackthorn.

brother, Robert, came up with the original idea about rebuilding Hackthorn, as he was a subscriber to the first volume, but he died sadly in 1787, at the young age of forty.

A fascinating tranche of documents relating to the building of the new hall survive in the family archive. These include James Lewis's presentation designs for the north and south fronts and plans for the basement and "Chamber" (that is, bedroom) floors. Lewis's original building contract, dated September 18, 1792, estimates the cost of building the new house at £5,006. This excludes "Fixtures, Carriage, Surveying and Traveling Charges" but does include such details as "enriched Cornice to Hall and Library and enriched Entablature to the Eating and Drawing Rooms" and mahogany doors on the ground floor. The "Best Stair Case" was to have a "Neat Mahogany Handrail" and "Iron Ballusters."

Inevitably, the final cost of the new house was much more than initially estimated; "Sundry Extra Works" are listed

in great detail on receipts made out to James Lewis between October 1795 and May 1796 amounting to a total of £1,424 16s 10½d. These extras include everything from "An Ornamental Ceiling in drawing Room" to a "Copper Cistern to Shower Bath" and a "Chopping block." Perhaps most revealing is John Cracroft's personal pocket account book, in which he writes: "Mr. Lewis's whole Acc't amounted to £7,355 1s 9d" beside the entry dated December 9, 1799. His son Robert Cracroft has scribbled a note in the margin: "I believe the total expense of House & Gardens was £10,000," along with a note to

ABOVE: *The staircase has a "Neat Mahogany Handrail" and "Iron Ballusters," as specified in the original building contract.*

OPPOSITE: *The library is bowed at one end and hung with family portraits above the bookcases.*

OVERLEAF: *A portrait of the heiress Elizabeth Amcotts hangs at one end of the drawing room.*

say the money his father owed James Lewis in 1801 was paid. There must have been a degree of friendship between John Cracroft and James Lewis by then, as John transferred a £400 interest in racehorses to Lewis in partial payment of the money he owed him, and in 1807 Lewis's daughter Eliza married John's second son, the Rev'd John Cracroft.

John Cracroft's new Hackthorn Hall is an elegant two-storey, square, neoclassical "villa," with five bays on the south and west fronts and three bays on the north (entrance) façade, below a balustraded cornice concealing attic windows. Inside, the rooms are pleasingly laid out around an oval staircase that rises

up beneath a glass skylight. The graceful balustrade, mentioned in the building contract, sweeps up the stone staircase and curves around on the landing, off of which bedroom apartments fan out. The curves of the staircase are echoed in the library, which is bowed at one end. Mahogany bookcases filled with leather-bound volumes line the walls beneath family portraits. A delicate neoclassical frieze of alternating urns and vases of fruit circles the room, and full-length windows have sweeping views down to the lake. Next door, the sun streams through the south-facing windows of the classically proportioned drawing room. The plasterwork ceiling is beautifully ornamented with a foliate rosette in a scalloped border and outer laurel medallion, with lozenge-filled panels at each end. A full-length portrait of Elizabeth Amcotts, Robert Cracroft's mother-in-law, depicted gliding through a wooded grove draped in a loosely fitted gown with her hair piled high on her head, hangs at one end of the room.

Evidently, the house was not big enough for later generations, as it was extended to the east in the mid-nineteenth century to accommodate a larger dining room with a canted bay window. The room has a coved ceiling and an arched sideboard recess and is hung with some fine family portraits, including three by Joseph Wright of Derby. A breakfast table stands in the bay window, which overlooks the serpentine pattern of intertwined box hedging that borders the gravel path leading to the church.

The gardens, laid out around the house, gently lead down to the lake and along the south side of the churchyard. "Lady's Walk" makes its way through woodland to the walled kitchen garden. It is named after Miss Ann Cracroft, who escaped down it when she eloped with her tutor, the Rev'd John Langhorne, translator of Plutarch's *Lives*.

ABOVE: *Charles Amcotts by Joseph Wright of Derby. A strong Jacobite, he was expelled from Cambridge for drinking the Pretender's health. He was later Member of Parliament for Boston in Lincolnshire.*

RIGHT: *The Cracroft family tree, which rolls up in a metal box complete with turning handle.*

OPPOSITE: *Robert Cracroft, resplendent in blue waistcoat, painted by Joseph Wright of Derby.*

Inside the walled garden is a glasshouse containing what is reputed to be the largest privately owned and second-oldest grapevine in Britain. The "Black Hamburg" vine was planted in 1868 by the head gardener, William Popple, and is the same variety as the Hampton Court vine (planted in 1768). Remarkably, it has been tended by only six gardeners in its life: Mr. Popple, Mr. Clarke, Mr. Richards, Mr. Moore, Mr. Bowen, and the present-day gardener, Mr. Donner.

The Gothic church now standing in the grounds was built between 1844 and 1849, funded chiefly by the lay rector, Charles Mainwaring, who was also the architect. It replaced an earlier church that had been "modernised and reduced in size" by John Cracroft. A church has been recorded at Hackthorn as far back as the Domesday Book (1086), and parts of the earlier church were incorporated into the present building. Tragically, Mainwaring died just before the new church furniture was finished. The carver, Mr Anstey, had been working on the furniture for five years at Mainwaring's home, and all of it was put up for sale by auction along with Mainwaring's other effects. As the lots came up, a tall Jewish dealer known as "Big Ben" stood up and announced to the amazed audience that he would buy them all for £10 and present them to the church, saying to the auctioneer: "Yes, Sir, I, a Jew, will present them myself to a Christian Temple." The furniture was duly installed in the church, leading the vicar to exclaim, "May the God of the Hebrews bless him for this act."

The west end of the church is dominated by the Cracroft family balcony, a throwback to more feudal times, when the squire and his family were segregated from the rest of the parishioners. The family could enter and exit discreetly via a small staircase and door leading directly into the garden.

Robert Cracroft Esq
of Hackthorn and
Whisby. Obiit 1763

ABOVE: *The dining room was added in the mid-nineteenth century.*

RIGHT: *A Victorian children's high chair stands in the dining room.*

OPPOSITE: *A path flanked by intertwined box hedging leads from the house to the church.*

OVERLEAF: *View of the altar from the church balcony.*

The current squire of Hackthorn is William Cracroft-Eley, who inherited the house from his mother, Bridget, and lives there with his wife and children. As Joint Master of the Burton Hunt, he is deeply rooted in rural affairs and has started his own company growing Miscanthus grass as an alternative energy source. The gardens have been superbly enhanced in recent years under the guidance of landscape architect Bunny Guinness, and the Hall is a much-loved family home; the future of Hackthorn looks bright.

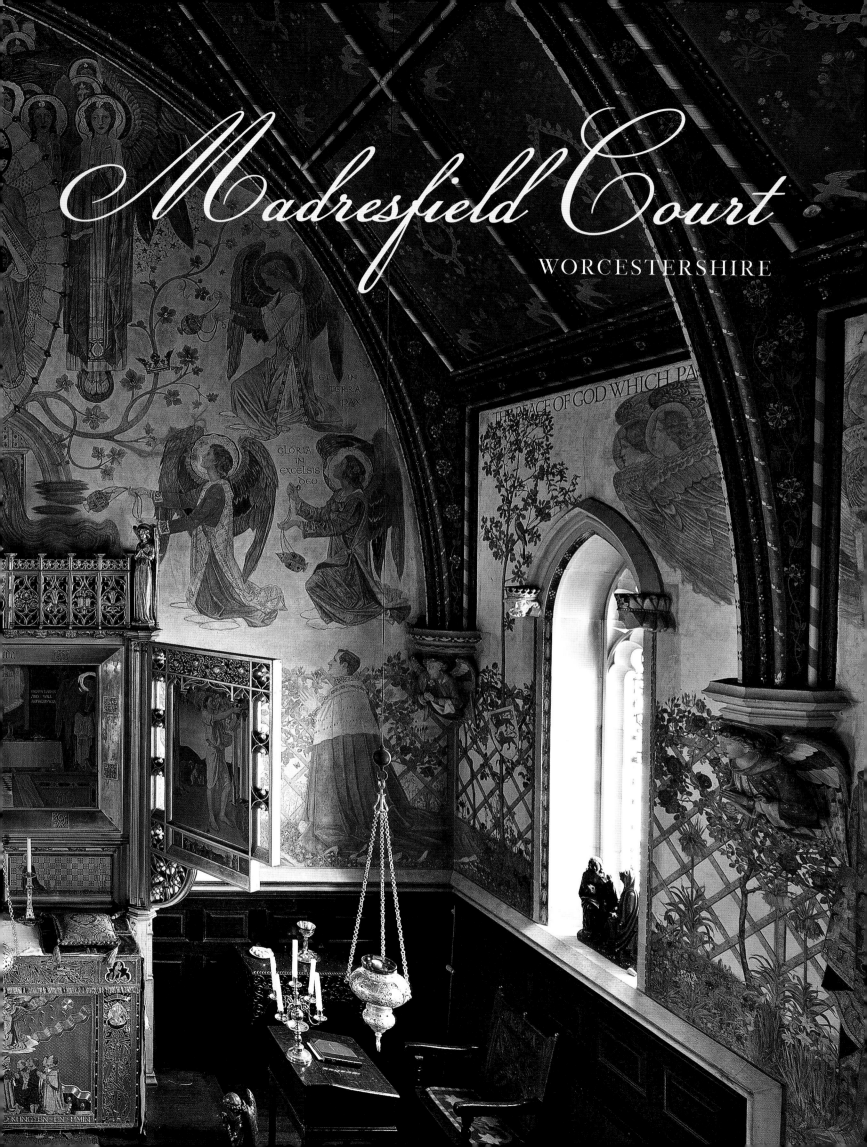

Madresfield Court

WORCESTERSHIRE

Evelyn Waugh wrote his novel Black Mischief *while staying at Madresfield in 1931. . . . Elements of Madresfield appear in Waugh's fictional house Hetton Grange in* A Handful of Dust, *also written during his "Madresfield period." When he came to write* Brideshead Revisited *more than a decade later, he drew inspiration from the Lygons for the main characters in the book, and the chapel at Brideshead is clearly modeled on the one at Madresfield.*

Madresfield is one of the most romantic country houses in England. Nestled at the foot of the gently undulating Malvern Hills, it has passed by inheritance for nearly a thousand years. The history of the generations that have lived within its walls, its architectural chronology, and its literary associations all make for a wonderful story peppered with adventure, scandal, and tragedy.

Old English for "Mower's Field," Madresfield was probably originally a wattle-and-daub manor house built by the de Bracy family, who settled on the lands soon after the Domesday Book was compiled in 1086. In 1196 Robert de Bracy dug a ditch around his house for defense—and no doubt drainage. Today, the house is still approached across a bridge over a wide moat, leading to a gatehouse. The gatehouse is mentioned in 1451, the year the widowed Isabel de Bracy retained the use of it when her grandson William Lygon was granted the house. In the

CATHERINE DENNE, COUNTESS BEAUCHAMP.
Sir William Beechey

WILLIAM, FIRST EARL BEAUCHAMP.
Sir William Beechey

OPPOSITE: *The anteroom links Tudor and Victorian Madresfield and leads the visitor from the entrance to the staircase hall. It is hung with tapestries and early portraits.*

FAR LEFT AND LEFT: *The Countess and first Earl Beauchamp by Sir William Beechey. He was made an earl in 1815 and chose the title after an ancestor, the second and last Lord Beauchamp, whose daughter had married Richard Lygon in the late fifteenth century.*

OVERLEAF: *The Gallery Court was created in the 1880s and is more like a medieval courtyard in Nuremberg than the court of an English country house. An open-air gallery runs along the east (right) side. The maze on the floor was inlaid in 1888.*

early sixteenth century, the Lygons extended the house and rebuilt the gatehouse in red brick. The house itself was further enlarged in 1593, the date inscribed over the entrance doorway. This Tudor house, which grew up around the medieval great hall, had a long gallery on the first floor. The house remained in essentially this form for just over two hundred years until a fortuitous inheritance enabled William Lygon, later first Earl Beauchamp, to extend the house by adding a classical wing in 1799, designed by architect George Byfield. This new box-like wing sat rather incongruously beside the ancient domain of the Lygons, the whole encircled by the moat.

When the fifth Earl Beauchamp inherited the house in 1863, he decided to rebuild it and give it a sense of unity. His architect was Philip Charles Hardwick, the fourth generation of an architectural dynasty and better known for his public buildings in the classical style. Hardwick had already designed some almshouses for the fourth earl the preceding year; he drew up his plans for Madresfield in the fashionable "Jacobethan" style during the winter of 1863–64. Just two years after the

work began, however, the fifth earl died at the young age of thirty-seven, and the baton passed to his younger brother, the sixth Earl Beauchamp. The completion of the work took another twenty-five years, during which time the old house was almost entirely rebuilt on more or less the original footprint. The result is a stupendous assemblage of gables, mullioned windows, steeply pitched roofs, and clusters of tall chimneypots topped by a wooden bell turret that could have come right out of *Grimms' Fairy Tales*; indeed, you might expect Rapunzel to let down her hair at any moment. The Gallery Court, over which the bell turret rises, could be mistaken for a courtyard in a medieval German town, complete with first-floor gallery open to the elements. It is overlooked by the dining room, a cavernous space with soaring hammer-beam roof, on the site of the original medieval great hall. Gothic tracery plate-glass windows, carved with heraldic ornament, flood the room with light; high up on the western wall is a stained-glass window depicting saints that gives the room an ecclesiastical air. Ranks of portraits line the walls, including a particularly fine

one of Queen Elizabeth I holding a sieve, a symbol of virginity. A minstrel's gallery runs across the east end.

Like the dining room, the long gallery was rebuilt by Hardwick, who retained its Elizabethan proportions but added a broad central bay overlooking the Moat Garden. In keeping with Victorian antiquarian taste, the fine carved-oak chimneypiece incorporates earlier carving dated 1610, which was removed from a farmhouse in Kempley, Gloucestershire. Early oak furniture jostles for position with display cabinets filled with curiosities brought back from the far reaches of the Empire. Next door in the New Gallery, a collection of arms and armour is displayed against the paneling below William Morris wallpaper. The heraldic stained-glass windows tint the sunlight as it streams through onto the polished surfaces of antique furniture.

The dawn of the twentieth century heralded further alterations to the house, this time in the Arts and Crafts idiom. The seventh Earl Beauchamp was, like his father, the sixth earl, a highly cultured and artistic patron. His wife, Lettice, sister of the second Duke of Westminster, had the chapel (built by Hardwick in 1867) decorated from top to bottom as a wedding present for

her husband. The wall decoration of idyllic pastoral scenes incorporates portraits of both Lord and Lady Beauchamp, as well as their seven children (added over a period of time), everything abounding in Christian symbolism. The murals were painted by Henry Payne with three student assistants. Payne also designed the stained glass. Reredos, side panels, candlesticks, balustrade, and organ case are all executed in true Arts and Crafts style.

PRECEDING PAGES LEFT:
The Countess Beauchamp in the chapel murals.

PRECEDING PAGES RIGHT, CLOCKWISE FROM TOP LEFT: *The gallery at the west end of the chapel was decorated by Henry Payne; Ladies Mary and Dorothy Lygon with an angel supposedly modeled on their nanny; the organ, by John Nicholson of Malvern, was decorated by Henry Payne; prayer books given by the seventh earl to his children, with their names embossed on the covers.*

RIGHT, OPPOSITE, AND OVERLEAF: *The staircase hall was constructed out of three rooms by the seventh earl. It is lit by three glass domes above a motto taken from Shelley's Adonais. The balusters are made from rock crystal.*

ONE REMAINS, THE MANU CHANGE

The seventh earl transformed three rooms at the center of the house into one dramatic, top-lit, double-height staircase hall. The staircase rises up one side of the room to a gallery that runs around two sides, its balusters made out of rock crystal. The library is also the seventh earl's creation, incorporating what had once been the billiard room to gain more space for the eight thousand or so books. He chose C. R. Ashbee and his Guild of Handicraft to carry out the work, which includes low-relief carvings of the Tree of Knowledge and the Tree of Life on the ends of two bookcases. The earl himself embroidered the Florentine flame-stitch covers on the chairs.

With nearly a thousand years of family occupancy, there are inevitably some family members who stand out. In the eighteenth century, Susannah Lygon's first cousin was the notorious William Jennens—the richest commoner in England. Despite his great wealth, he was incredibly stingy and known as "the miser." When he died in 1798, Susannah's son was one of three beneficiaries; the inheritance enabled the family to purchase an earldom and extend Madresfield.

As Jennens had died intestate, the inheritance was disputed in a court case that lasted 117 years and was said to have been the inspiration for the case of Jarndyce v. Jarndyce in Charles Dickens's *Bleak House.*

The sixth Earl Beauchamp, in addition to holding government office, was a distinguished churchman and theological scholar and was closely involved with the Oxford movement, which in part helped to found Keble College, Oxford. His daughter Mary was a pupil and friend of Edward Elgar. The thirteenth of Elgar's *Enigma Variations* was dedicated to Mary and recalls her voyage to Australia, where she had gone to act as hostess for her brother the seventh earl, when he was made Governor of New South Wales. Like his father, the seventh earl held public office and became Lord Warden of the Cinque Ports. At court he was appointed Lord Steward of the Royal Household, bore the Sword of State at George V's coronation, and in 1914 was made a Knight of the Garter. Despite these prestigious positions and the duties of high political office in the Liberal government, he was a deeply devoted and loving father to his seven children and they

174

HADOWS FLU: LIFE LIKE A DOME OF MANU COLOVRED GLASS STAINS THE W

THE ONE REMAINS, THE MANY CHANGE AND PA...

IT TO FRAGMENTS

in turn adored him. Still lying on the front pew in the chapel are the leather-bound prayer books he commissioned specially for each of them, tenderly inscribed on the title page with a personal dedication.

Tragically, the domestic bliss at Madresfield and the seventh earl's glittering career were both cut short when he became embroiled in a homosexual scandal that forced him into exile abroad for nearly the rest of his life. His vindictive brother-in-law Bend'or, the Duke of Westminster, threatened legal action against him and exposure in the press, with the inevitable shame it would bring on the family. Bend'or forced his sister to leave the earl and come and live on his Cheshire estate, taking with her Richard, the youngest of the Lygon children. The other children faithfully stood by their father and initially took turns visiting him so that he was never alone, whether in Paris, Sydney, San Francisco, or Venice. The charges against him were finally dropped six years later and he returned home to his beloved Madresfield, only to die of cancer just over a year later.

Several of the children of the seventh Earl Beauchamp were friends of the young Evelyn Waugh, who was at Oxford with Hugh Lygon. Waugh wrote his novel *Black Mischief* while staying at Madresfield in 1931 and dedicated it to Hugh's sisters Mary and Dorothy. Elements of Madresfield appear in Waugh's fictional house Hetton Grange in *A Handful of Dust*, also written during his "Madresfield period." When he came to write *Brideshead Revisited* more than a decade later, he drew inspiration from the Lygons for the main characters in the book, and the chapel at Brideshead is clearly modeled on the one at Madresfield.

Today, Madresfield is the home of Lucy Chenevix-Trench, great-niece of the last Earl Beauchamp, her husband, Jonathan, and their four young children. For the first time in a hundred years, the rooms are alive again with the shouts of little ones. The house has recently undergone extensive renovations, including the creation of a family kitchen, stylishly integrating the needs of twenty-first-century life into a historic house that will ensure its survival into the future.

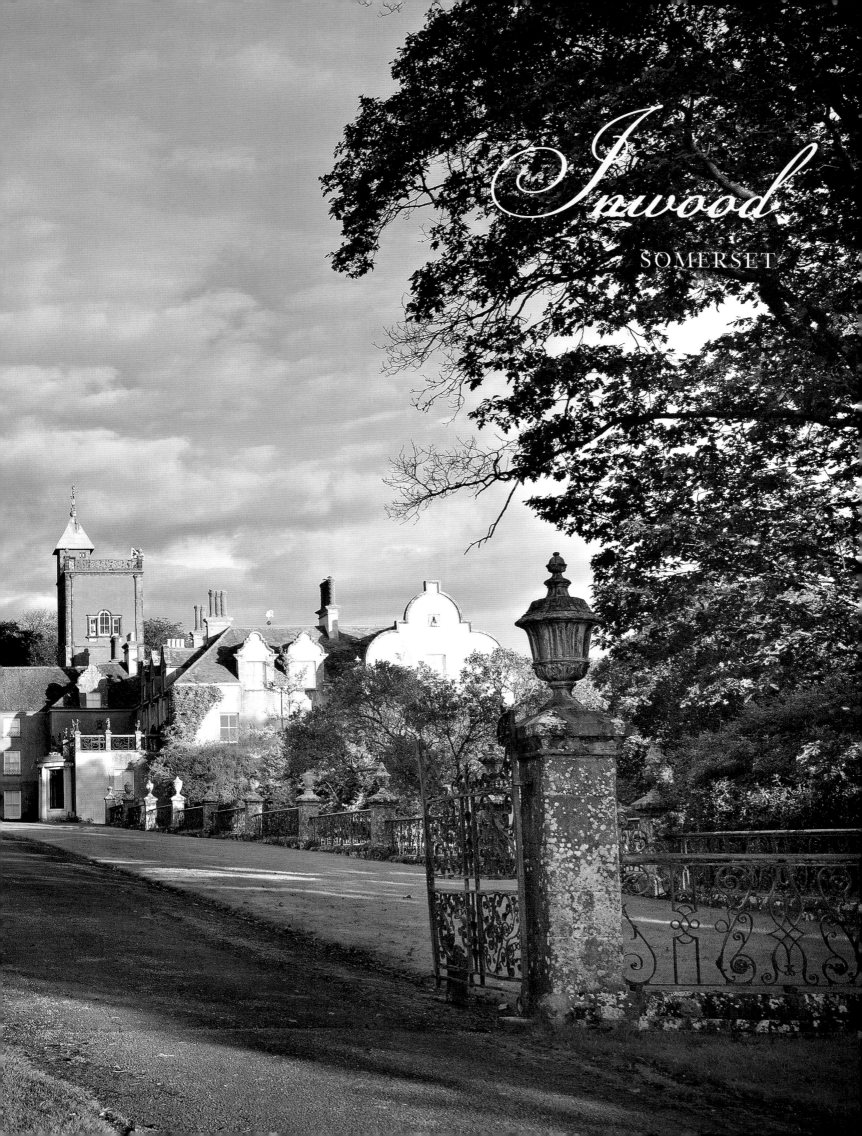

Inwood

SOMERSET

Nothing prepares the visitor for what lies inside the relatively plain exterior of Inwood. Merthyr and Lady Theodora clearly enjoyed collecting and they displayed their collections against an extraordinary backdrop. . . . A whole room is papered in Chinese wallpaper and filled with Chinese, Japanese, and chinoiserie furniture, objects, and pictures beneath a rococo plasterwork ceiling. In the main gallery, . . . fine ceramics sit on every surface and inside every cabinet.

PRECEDING PAGES: *The front drive with the sun catching the classical tower and Dutch gables. As its name suggests, Inwood is surrounded by woodland and completely hidden from the outside world. The great stable block lies to the left, behind the trees.*

OPPOSITE: *View from the gallery into the library. The paneling is eighteenth century and was incorporated into the house in the late nineteenth century. The pair of Chinese Export vases is one of the many treasures collected by Merthyr and Lady Theodora Guest in the late nineteenth century.*

Inwood is an enchanted domain, the product of a union between two great nineteenth-century dynasties: the Grosvenors and the Guests. In 1877 Thomas Merthyr Guest, second son of Sir Josiah Guest, Baronet, married Lady Theodora Grosvenor, ninth and youngest daughter of the second Marquess of Westminster. The Guests were leading industrialists whose fortune was based on the manufacture of iron in South Wales. The Grosvenors were one of the richest landowning families in the country, primarily as a result of owning large parts of central London, including Mayfair and Belgravia. When the marriage was announced, letters of congratulation poured in, not only from leading members of society but also from members of the British royal family and crowned heads of Europe. As the youngest child, Lady Theodora was a particular favourite of her mother, by then the Dowager Marchioness of Westminster and herself a member of one of Britain's leading dynasties, the Leveson-Gowers, Dukes of Sutherland. Through these great marriage alliances, Lady Theodora and her husband were related to or connected with much of the British aristocracy, including many of its dukes.

Both Merthyr Guest (he was known by his middle name, taken from Merthyr Tydfil,

the town in South Wales where the family fortunes were based) and Lady Theodora were passionate about fox hunting; they are said to have first met on the hunting field in Dorset. After her father's death, Lady Theodora's mother had moved to Motcombe, an estate in Dorset that she had for her lifetime. Merthyr's family also lived in Dorset, at Canford Manor, purchased by his father and mother, the beautiful Lady Charlotte Bertie, in 1846.

The newlyweds lived for the first two years after their marriage at the recently built Barcote Manor in Oxfordshire, a substantial Tudor Revival mansion. Oxfordshire was not to their liking, however, and they returned to the West Country, intent on building a house fit for the daughter of a marquess. Here, on the border of Somerset and Dorset, they bought Inwood, a small Regency villa owned by Colonel John Glossop, located, as the name suggests, in its own wooded oasis.

The house was almost completely rebuilt in 1879, subsuming Colonel Glossop's villa. As their abiding passion was fox hunting, a great stable block was erected in 1880–81, complete with kennels for the foxhounds. No architect is credited with the rebuilding of the house and it is believed that Merthyr acted as his own architect, although he must

have had a talented clerk of works to turn his vision into reality. Through his connections in the industrial world, he undoubtedly had access to the very latest technology, even though the style of the house betrays an amateur hand. Early photographs reveal that the house went through two phases of construction. The first resulted in a loosely classical mansion of irregular form, part two-storey, part three-storey, the high-pitched roof pierced with dormer windows and crowned with tall chimneys. To one side was a two-storey rectangular window bay with triple-light windows. Most bizarre of all was a circular turret with pointed roof tacked onto the side of the house. Just visible in the background is the great red brick tower that still stands at the back of the house. Like the house, it was given a somewhat classical air with a Palladian window on each side above much larger, dressed-stone "blind" Palladian windows. Dated in brick 1881, together with the initials of Merthyr, Lady Theodora, and their daughter, Elizabeth, the tower remains unaltered. From the top of its copper-roofed stair turret, it commands magnificent views

OPPOSITE: *The tower houses a trove of objects from all over the world; every cupboard opens to reveal another collection.*

TOP LEFT: *Miss Guest as a child. Inwood was built by her parents.*

BOTTOM LEFT: *Inwood after the first phase of construction and before the Dutch gables and gallery wing were added. Note the curious circular turret with pointed roof on the right.*

OVERLEAF: *The tower, built in 1881, affords magnificent views of the Vale of Blackmore. The initials of Merthyr Guest, his wife, Lady Theodora, and their daughter, Elizabeth, are found in the brickwork.*

over the surrounding Blackmore Vale, prime hunting country to this day.

The second construction phase enlarged the house considerably and gave it essentially the appearance we see today. A large projecting wing was added to the southeast

front; it comprises an L-shaped gallery with three grand reception rooms leading off it. The corner turret seems to have been retained and incorporated into the new wing by running it the full height of the building, lending Inwood a quirky Scottish Baronial air. The new wing and all of the dormer windows were given Dutch gables and the whole building was rendered in grey, reinforcing the Scottish feeling. Perhaps it was a nod to Lady Theodora's mother's illustrious Scottish descent via the Sutherlands and their great ducal seat, Dunrobin Castle.

The Dowager Marchioness of Westminster spent much of her time at Inwood with her favourite daughter and even had her own rooms. A large conversation piece by Frederick George Cotman, hanging in pride of place in the dining room, shows her playing dummy whist with her daughter and son-in-law. This picture and the charming full-length portrait of Merthyr and Lady Theodora's daughter, Elizabeth, were both exhibited at the Royal Academy in 1882. When the marchioness died in 1891, she left

TOP: *Inwood after the second phase of building. The Dowager Marchioness of Westminster is being pulled in a Bath chair in the foreground.*

ABOVE: *The view from the top of the tower looking down the front drive.*

RIGHT: *Lady Theodora and Merthyr Guest playing dummy whist with her mother, the Dowager Marchioness of Westminster. The marchioness had her own rooms at Inwood.*

OPPOSITE: *One of the many fox hunting trophies at Inwood, displayed on the dining table.*

her entire "widow's portion" of £195,000 to Theodora, causing a huge family rift with her brother, by then ennobled as the first Duke of Westminster. He took his sister to court but failed to win the case and what he saw as his siblings' share of the inheritance.

Nothing prepares the visitor for what lies inside the relatively plain exterior of Inwood. Merthyr and Lady Theodora clearly enjoyed collecting and they displayed their collections against an extraordinary backdrop. Some of the interior fittings, including doors, paneling, and chimneypieces, appear to have been removed from other buildings and incorporated into the new house. Exuberant Chinese Chippendale carving on a mirrored background lines the walls of the upstairs gallery overlooking the floor below. A whole room is papered in Chinese wallpaper and filled with Chinese, Japanese, and chinoiserie furniture, objects, and pictures beneath a rococo plasterwork ceiling. The Kentian paneling and stone mantelpiece in the main gallery are said to have come from a London mansion, demolished when Inwood was

being built. Fine ceramics sit on every surface and inside every cabinet, some of which might have been inherited from Merthyr's mother, the great porcelain collector Lady Charlotte Schreiber. She had caused a society scandal in 1855 when she married Merthyr's childhood tutor, Charles Schreiber (his own father had died in 1840). Old Master pictures vie for space with family portraits and hunting pictures.

That fox hunting was the couple's chief pleasure is reflected in much of what they collected. They commissioned many hunting paintings from Basil Nightingale, who depicted not only hunting scenes but also studies of favourite horses and hounds. The main bedroom corridor is lined with horse paintings by Claude Lorraine Ferneley set into the paneling. Merthyr started collecting the hunt buttons from every hunt in the country. He also wrote to every famous huntsman and offered to send him a new hunting horn in exchange for his old one; the result is a unique collection of hunting horns. Merthyr kept his own pack of foxhounds at

Inwood and all of his horses were grey—at one point there were eighty grey horses in the stables. When the hunting season ended, the couple traveled widely on the Continent and in America; Lady Theodora recorded the places she visited in delicate watercolors. Merthyr had his own yacht and every August they sailed to Norway to enjoy the fishing on the Namsen River, where he advised the locals to cast aside their nets and catch salmon with a rod and line as he did.

After the deaths of Merthyr (1904) and Lady Theodora (1924), Inwood was left to their only child, Elizabeth Augusta, who was named after her godmother, the Duchess of Cambridge. Known to all as Aura, she added to the estate considerably. Like her parents, she was passionate about fox hunting, having previously hunted with beagles and buckhounds. A master of foxhounds for fifty years, she later became Master of the Blackmore Vale foxhounds, and it was through a shared interest in fox hunting that she developed a close friendship with a young French aristocrat, Comte Guy de Pelet, who was living in England. In the absence of any direct family of her own, she decided to leave the estate to him. Thus his eldest son, Richard, was christened with the middle name Grosvenor to carry on the family line. When Elizabeth died in 1960, Comte de Pelet and his family moved into Inwood. The comte cherished this valuable legacy, which, after his death, was passed on to Richard, his wife, Isabel, and their children. A former director of Christie's and chairman of the Blackmore and Sparkford Vale foxhounds, Richard is an entirely fitting squire of Inwood, and the rooms regularly reverberate with the sounds of revelry, as guests gather for family and hunt parties. Long may the de Pelets live at Inwood, there "by virtue not by pedigree," as the Grosvenor family motto says.

PRECEDING PAGES LEFT: *The drawing room is furnished with Victorian painted-satinwood furniture and Old Master pictures.*

PRECEDING PAGES RIGHT, CLOCKWISE FROM TOP LEFT: *Letters of congratulation to Lady Theodora Grosvenor on her engagement to Merthyr Guest; a Chinese Chippendale overmantel mirror in the drawing room; writing implements and old letters in the drawing room; a magnificent view of Venice hangs over a French Boulle commode.*

OPPOSITE TOP: *The drive sweeps through well-wooded parkland.*

OPPOSITE BOTTOM: *Heraldic beasts surmount the pillars of the Lion Gate.*

TOP LEFT: *The Chinese tea pavilion in the garden.*

BOTTOM LEFT: *The old water tower, designed in a medieval style, is now used as an apple storehouse.*

Rodmarton

GLOUCESTERSHIRE

The importance of Rodmarton as a superb example of the Arts and Crafts movement cannot be overstated. . . . As C. R. Ashbee, who established the Guild of Handicraft at Chipping Campden in 1902, wrote after visiting Rodmarton in 1914: "I've seen no modern work equal to it, nothing I know of Lutyens or Baker comes up to it. . . . The Eng[lish] Arts and Crafts Movement at its best is here—so are the vanishing traditions of the Cotswolds."

Rodmarton is one of the finest Arts and Crafts houses, fully realizing the vision of its enlightened owners, Claud and Margaret Biddulph. Built over a period of twenty years, it is hard to believe that this many-gabled manor house with its embracing wings is not even a hundred years old.

At about 500 acres, Rodmarton formed but a part of the much larger Kemble estate, which was inherited by Claud's father, the first Lord Biddulph, from Anna Gordon. Kemble went to Claud's elder brother, John, and Claud, who worked for the family bank, Gordon, Askew, & Biddulph, was given the Rodmarton estate by his father in 1894. Although there had been a manor house at Rodmarton in earlier times, sited near the church, it had fallen into ruin by 1796. Lacking a house of any great size, Claud and Margaret decided to build a new one on a virgin site with wide sweeping views across to the Berkshire Downs.

The Biddulphs chose as their architect Ernest Barnsley, a talented idealist who had moved out of London to the Cotswolds with his brother, Sidney, a furniture maker, and Ernest Gimson, an architect and craftsman. For followers of the Arts and Crafts movement, the Cotswolds was a mecca where traditional crafts still flourished and the industrial world they so loathed

seemed far away. Work started in 1909 and continued until the outbreak of World War I. Everything—inside and out—was built by hand, using materials sourced from the estate and local labour whenever possible. The Biddulphs consulted contemporary publications on house building, one of which was *Modern Homes; selected examples of dwelling houses, described and illustrated by T. Raffles Davison* (1909). In this book they added their own annotations in pencil,

PRECEDING PAGES: *View of the Troughery Garden, where old stone feeding troughs mingle with topiary.*

OPPOSITE: *A pair of red-painted traveling chests stands in the hall. They were designed by Peter Waals, made by Owen Scrubey, and painted by Alfred and Louise Powell.*

LEFT: *An oak children's "punishment" chair, designed by Sidney Barnsley and intended to make small children sit up straight.*

including alterations to Lutyens's plan of Marsh Court, which is indeed similar to that executed at Rodmarton.

The house was built in roughly three stages, each bigger than the last, starting with the service wing at the east end, proceeding to the family living rooms, and finishing with the main part of the house, where the chapel wing terminates the west end. Traditional Cotswold features were used in abundance: local stone, stone tiles, pointed gables, stone mullions, leaded windows, and tall chimneys. A temporary railway line brought the stone from a nearby quarry and timber, mainly oak, was felled on the estate. Norman Jewson (who married Ernest Barnsley's daughter in 1911) designed the lead work with its charming detailing. Work resumed after the war in 1918, and the house was finally finished in 1929. By then Ernest Barnsley had died, so it was left to his son-in-law Norman Jewson to oversee its completion.

As much care was lavished on Rodmarton's interiors as on its architecture. Much of the furniture and metalwork was made in the estate workshop, with the Arts and Crafts ideals clearly at the forefront of everyone's minds. Sidney Barnsley designed and made some of the pieces, including the

oak dining table with its distinctive hayrake stretcher. Ernest Gimson also designed some pieces, though they were actually executed by his foreman, Peter Waals, at the Daneway workshop Gimson had set up with the Barnsleys in 1902. Waals, a gifted Dutch cabinetmaker, was responsible for making much of the furniture at Rodmarton, including Margaret Biddulph's walnut drop-front secrétaire with checkered banding of holly and ebony and exposed dovetail joints, a characteristic of Arts and Crafts furniture.

Gimson also designed the metalwork, which was executed by his gifted protégé, the blacksmith Alfred Bucknell, along with Fred and Frank Baldwin, who were based at the Rodmarton Forge. The work ranged from ornate fixtures, such as the sconces in the dining room and the fire irons and spark guard in the library, to all of the window casements, which were made by hand.

Gimson was skilled in plasterwork as well, although at Rodmarton, with its predominantly whitewashed walls and exposed timber beams, restraint was the order of the day. Some of the walls were adorned with murals by Hilda Benjamin; one on the stairs depicts the Biddulphs' daughter, Marnie, at age nine. Other walls

Opposite top: *The entrance (north) front with wings that seem to embrace the visitor.*

Opposite bottom: *The south front overlooking the terrace. The yew hedges were planted in the 1930s.*

Left: *One of the bay windows in the library.*

Below: *Claud and Margaret Biddulph, the builders of Rodmarton.*

Bottom: *In the dining room the oak tables were designed by Sidney Barnsley; the larger one was executed by Peter Waals.*

PAGE 212, TOP: *The stone tablet above the front door bears the date 1916.*

PAGE 212, BOTTOM LEFT AND RIGHT: *Lead work with charming details of animals, designed by Norman Jewson.*

PAGE 213, TOP: *The library was originally the ballroom. Louise Powell painted the blue screen; Ernest Gimson designed the rocking chairs.*

PAGE 213, BOTTOM LEFT AND RIGHT: *A 1926 Blüthner grand piano and stool, whimsically painted by Louise Powell.*

PAGES 214-15: *The drawing room was originally a crafts studio. The large chest in the foreground is an early work by Sidney Barnsley.*

ABOVE: *The metalwork and all of the wooden items in the chapel were made in the Rodmarton workshop.*

OPPOSITE: *An appliqué hanging by the Rodmarton Women's Guild depicts the Coronation of George VI in 1937.*

OVERLEAF: *The gardens at Rodmarton are justifiably famous.*

PAGES 220-21: *The Troughery Garden.*

were covered with appliqué wall hangings made by the Rodmarton Women's Guild, many of whom lived in the village. Hilda Benjamin designed the hangings, and she included portraits of many of the villagers in them. When the house was first built, the drawing room was used as a workroom for the villagers, who were not only skilled in embroidery and needlework but also turned their hands to cane work.

Ceramics specially commissioned for the house were painted by Alfred Powell and his wife, Louise. The couple also painted some of the furniture—both the spinet and the grand piano were delicately decorated with trailing flowers. In the chapel, Edward Payne executed two circular stained-glass panels, one with the coat of arms of Claud Biddulph and the other with his wife's (the Howard arms).

Barnsley put as much attention into the layout of the garden as he did into the house, and its fame continues to grow as each successive generation of the Biddulph family treasures and enhances it. Taking full advantage of its south-facing orientation, Barnsley designed the garden as a series of outdoor rooms, enabling the coexistence of

a great variety of planting schemes. The impressive topiary, now enjoyed by visitors, is the result of nearly a century of growth; the borders, terminating in a charming garden house with pyramidal roof, are another key feature. Not surprisingly, the original head gardener, William Scrubey, is commemorated in a stone inscription over the doorway to the garden: "W Scrubey Hortorum Cultor." Architect Ernest Barnsley and the foreman of the Rodmarton workshop, Alfred Wright, are also honored, accompanied by an extract from Oliver Goldsmith's poem "Deserted Village" celebrating wholesome labour.

The importance of Rodmarton as a superb example of the Arts and Crafts movement cannot be overstated, and it is still cherished and lovingly maintained by the Biddulph family. As C. R. Ashbee, who established the Guild of Handicraft at Chipping Campden in 1902, wrote after visiting Rodmarton in 1914: "I've seen no modern work equal to it, nothing I know of Lutyens or Baker comes up to it.... The Eng[lish] Arts and Crafts Movement at its best is here—so are the vanishing traditions of the Cotswolds."

SELECTED BIBLIOGRAPHY

GENERAL

Bateman, John. *The Great Landowners of Great Britain and Ireland: A List of All Owners of Three Thousand Acres and Upwards.* 4th ed. London: Harrison, 1883.

Burke, Sir Bernard, and Ashworth P. Burke. *A Genealogical and Heraldic History of the Landed Gentry of Great Britain.* London: Harrison, 1906.

Cokayne, George Edward, et al. *The Complete Peerage.* Reprint. Gloucester, UK: Alan Sutton Publishing, 1987.

Colvin, Howard. *A Biographical Dictionary of British Architects, 1600–1840.* 4th ed. New Haven and London: Yale University Press, 2008.

Girouard, Mark. *Life in the English Country House: A Social and Architectural History.* New Haven and London: Yale University Press, 1978.

Harris, Eileen. *British Architectural Books and Writers 1556–1785.* Cambridge, UK: Cambridge University Press, 1990.

Harris, John, Roy Strong, and Marcus Binney, eds. *The Destruction of the Country House 1875–1975.* London: Thames & Hudson, 1974.

Miers, Mary, et al. *The English Country House: From the Archives of Country Life.* New York: Rizzoli, 2009.

Mosley, Charles, ed. *Burke's Peerage & Baronetage.* 2 vols. 106th ed. Switzerland: Morris Genealogical Books, 1999.

Musson, Jeremy. *English Country House Interiors.* New York: Rizzoli, 2011.

Nicolson, Adam. *The Gentry: Stories of the English.* London: Harper Press, 2011.

Robinson, John Martin. *Felling the Ancient Oaks: How England Lost Its Great Country Estates.* London: Aurum, 2012.

Townend, Peter, ed. *Burke's Genealogical and Heraldic History of the Landed Gentry.* Vol. 1. 18th ed. London: Burke's Peerage Ltd, 1965.

BADMINTON

Flower, Sibylla Jane. *The Stately Homes of Britain.* London: Debrett's Peerage, 1982, pp. 132–43.

Foss, Arthur. *The Dukes of Britain.* London: Herbert Press, 1986, pp. 41–47.

Harris, John. *Badminton: The Duke of Beaufort, his House.* Privately published guidebook, 2007.

Hussey, Christopher. *English Country Houses: Early Georgian 1715–1760.* Woodbridge, UK: Antique Collectors' Club, 1953, pp. 161–66.

Jackson-Stops, Gervase. "Badminton, Gloucestershire." *Country Life,* 9 April 1987, pp. 128–31, and 16 April 1987, pp. 136–39.

Mander, Nicholas. *Country Houses of the Cotswolds: From the Archives of Country Life.* London: Aurum, 2008, pp. 104–11.

Moore, Derry (photographs), and Mitchell Owens (text). *In House.* New York: Rizzoli, 2009, pp. 132–47.

EUSTON HALL

Oswald, Arthur. "Euston Hall, Suffolk," *Country Life,* 10 January 1957, pp. 58–61; 17 January 1957, pp. 102–5; and 24 January 1957, pp. 148–51.

GOODWOOD HOUSE

Baird, Rosemary. *Goodwood: Art and Architecture, Sport and Family.* London: Frances Lincoln, 2007. See pp. 229–31 for a list of other publications on Goodwood.

HACKTHORN HALL

Shields, Steffie. "Hackthorn Harvest" [gardens only]. *Lincolnshire Life*, October 2010, pp. 34–36.

INWOOD

"Inwood House, Somerset" [gardens only]. *Country Life*, 27 July 1901, pp. 112–17.

KENTCHURCH COURT

The Artist and the Country House from the Fifteenth Century to the Present Day. Exh. cat. Sotheby's London, December 1995. London: Sotheby's, p. 25.

Cornforth, John. "Kentchurch Court, Herefordshire." *Country Life*, 15 December 1966, pp. 1632–37; 22 December 1966, pp. 1688–91; and 29 December 1966, pp. 1734–37.

Reid, Peter. *Burke's and Savills Guide to Country Houses*. Vol. 2. *Herefordshire, Shropshire, Warwickshire, Worcestershire*. London: Burke's Peerage, Ltd, 1980, pp. 40–41.

MADRESFIELD COURT

Aslet, Clive. "Madresfield Court, Worcestershire." *Country Life*, 16 October 1980, pp. 1338–41; 23 October 1980, pp. 1458–61; and 30 October 1980, pp. 1551–55.

———. *The Arts & Crafts Country House: From the Archives of Country Life*. London: Aurum, 2011, pp. 91–95.

de la Cour, John. *Madresfield Court*. Privately published guidebook.

Girouard, Mark. *Enthusiasms*. London: Frances Lincoln, 2011, pp. 112–26.

Lyttelton, Celia. "Madresfield Court." *The World of Interiors*, March 2009, pp. 110–23.

"Madresfield Court, Worcestershire." *Country Life*, 30 March 1907, pp. 450–60.

Mulvagh, Jane. *Madresfield: One Home, One Family, One Thousand Years*. London: Doubleday, 2008.

MILTON

A. D. "Milton, Northamptonshire." *Country Life*, 9 November 1912, pp. 638–48.

Bailey, Catherine. *Black Diamonds*. London: Penguin, 2008.

Harris, John. *Sir William Chambers: Knight of the Polar Star*. London: A. Zwemmer Ltd., 1970, pp. 238–39, figs. 87, 89.

Hussey, Christopher. "Milton, Northamptonshire." *Country Life*, 18 May 1961, pp. 1148–51; 25 May 1961, pp. 1210–13; and 1 June 1961, pp. 1270–74.

Worsley, Giles. "Fashion's Most Dedicated Follower." *Country Life*, 26 July 2001, pp. 67.

PRIDEAUX PLACE

Goodall, John. "Prideaux Place, Cornwall." *Country Life*, 9 June 2010, pp. 80–85, and 16 June 2010, 106–11.

RODMARTON MANOR

Aslet, Clive. "Rodmarton Manor, Gloucestershire." *Country Life*, 19 October 1978, pp. 1178–81, and 26 October 1978, pp. 1298–1302.

———. *The Arts & Crafts Country House: From the Archives of Country Life*. London: Aurum, 2011, pp. 102–9.

Mander, Nicholas. *Country Houses of the Cotswolds: From the Archives of Country Life*. London: Aurum, 2008, pp. 174–79.

Moore, Derry (photographs), and Mitchell Owens (text). *In House*, New York: Rizzoli, 2009, pp. 166–69.

Oswald, Arthur. "Rodmarton, Gloucestershire." *Country Life*, 4 April 1931, pp. 422–27.

Venison, Tony. "'Successions of Outdoor Rooms,' Rodmarton Manor Garden, Gloucestershire." *Country Life*, 16 December 1976, pp. 1844–46.

For Olda,
in memory of
Desmond FitzGerald, 29th Knight of Glin

ACKNOWLEDGMENTS

The Duke and Duchess of Beaufort, Simon Biddulph, John and Sarah Biddulph, Frances Buckle, Linda Campbell, Jonathan and Lucy Chenevix-Trench, Lawrence Clarke, Penny Cracroft-Amcotts, William and Maggie Cracroft-Eley, Joanna Fennell, the Duke and Duchess of Grafton, the Dowager Duchess of Grafton, John and Eileen Harris, Tim Knox, Johnny and Jan Lucas-Scudamore, Rosie Lucas-Scudamore, the Earl and Countess of March and Kinrara, Sir Philip Naylor-Leyland, Bt and Lady Isabella Naylor-Leyland, Tom and Alice Naylor-Leyland, the Duke and Duchess of Richmond and Gordon, Susan Palmer, Saskia Peill, Comte and Comtesse Richard de Pelet, Charlie and Fiona de Pelet, Sarah Pope, Peter and Elisabeth Prideaux-Brune, Nicholas and Martha Prideaux-Brune, Orlando Rock, Rupert Uloth, Edward Wortley.

—JAMES PEILL

All of the houses are privately owned. Euston Hall, Goodwood House, Kentchurch Court, Prideaux Place, and Rodmarton Manor are open to the public on a regular basis. Badminton, Hackthorn Hall, Inwood, Madresfield Court, and Milton are not open to the public.

First published in the United States of America in 2013 by
The Vendome Press
1334 York Avenue
New York, NY 10021
www.vendomepress.com

Photographs copyright © 2013 James Fennell
Text copyright © 2013 James Peill
Foreword copyright © 2013 Julian Fellowes
Copyright © 2013 The Vendome Press

ISBN 978-0-86565-306-1

Editor: Jacqueline Decter
Production Editor: Alecia Reddick
Designer: Patricia Fabricant

Library of Congress Cataloging-in-Publication Data

Peill, James.
The English country house / by James Peill ; photographs by James Fennell ;
foreword by Julian Fellowes.
pages cm
ISBN 978-0-86565-306-1 (hardback)
I. Fennell, James. II. Fellowes, Julian. III. Title.
NA7620.P45 2013
747--dc23
2013016113

Printed in China by OGI
First printing

PRECEDING PAGES: *Details of bookshelves in the library at Prideaux Place.*

THIS PAGE: *Detail of the King's Bed at Goodwood, made using the ambassadorial hangings of the third Duke of Richmond.*